YORUBA PO[illegible]

BAYREUTH

African Studies Series

Publisher/Editor:
Eckhard Breitinger
Bayreuth University
D-95440 Bayreuth
Germany /R.F.A
www.breitinger.org

Die Deutsche Bibliothek – CIP Einheitstitelaufnahme.
Ein Titeldatensatz für diese Publikation ist bei der
Deutschen Bibliothek erhältlich.

Price per copy: € 12.95 plus postage

ISBN 3-927510-75-0

ISSN 0178-0034

Printed by D. Gräbner, D- 96146 Altendorf

YORUBA POETRY

Compiled and edited by
Ulli Beier
with Timi Laoye I, Bakare Gbadamosi,
Duro Ladipo and Ademola Onibonokuta

Bayreuth African Studies 62

ACKNOWLEDGEMENTS

This book is an enlarged and revised version of *Yoruba Poetry*, Cambridge UP 1970. A short essay on the origin of this book has been added and the "Notes" have been rewritten. The section on "Medicinal herbs", contributed to the former volume by Pierre Verger, has been omitted here because in 1995, Verger's comprehensive collection of songs of medicinal herbs was published post mortem (*Ewe*, Sao Paolo/Brazil: Odebrecht).

The English renderings in this volume were made by the following:

Timi Laoye I and Ulli Beier: "The Timi of Ede", "I am blessing two, not one", "The sky is immense, but grows no grass", "The river is flowing, the river is going", "I say arise" and "Woru".

Duro Ladipo and Ulli Beier: "Shango" and "The Alafin of Oyo".

Ademola Onibonokuta and Ulli Beier: all the poems in the section "Magic formulas".

Bolaji Idowu: "Young ones never hear the death of cloth".

All other poems were collected and translated by Bakare Gbadamosi and Ulli Beier.

CONTENTS

ON TRANSLATING YORUBA POETRY

Nobody who attempts to translate Yoruba into English will doubt that 'poetry is what is left out in translation'. For the music inherent in this language is something no rendering, however clever, can possibly attempt. The Yoruba organist E.K. Phillips describes his language as the missing link between music and speech.

Yoruba is a tonal language. That is, each word has to be pronounced with its proper tone pattern: each syllable can have a high, mid or low tone or could be pronounced on one of several glides. A change in tones may make the word unintelligible or may, in several cases, even give it a different meaning. Words with two meanings are common, like *koríko*, 'grass' and *kòrikò*, 'hyena'. Some have three meanings, like *ìlú*, 'town'; *ìlù*, 'drum'; *ìlu*, 'gimlet'. In addition, some have many meanings, like:

àgbọ̀n	chin
àgbọn	coconut
agbọ̀n	basket
agbọ́n	wasp
àgbộn	the heat of pepper.

Mostly the meanings seem entirely unrelated, but occasionally one gets combinations like *ọkọ*, 'husband'; *ọkọ́*, 'hoe'; *ọ̀kọ̀*, 'spear', where related meanings seem differentiated by tones. The translator has no hope of reproducing the type of subtle play that is possible with such meanings, and there is no hope of finding equivalents for the music of words like:

kọ́lọ́kọ́lọ́	stealthily
kọ́lọkọ̀lọ	circuitously
kọ̀lọ̀kọ́lọ́	muddy
kọ̀lọ̀kọ̀lọ̀	fox

When one has heard hunters communicate with each other across long distances in the forest, one begins to understand the extraordinary carrying power of this language. European consonant clusters and indefinite vowel sounds would get lost in the winds, whereas Yoruba with only seven vowels (a, i, e, ẹ, o, ọ, u) and syllables that consist usually of one consonant followed by a vowel or of a vowel by itself, remains intelligible over a long distance.

It is this tonal quality of Yoruba and its vowel structure that enables the drummer to recite poetry. The Yoruba *dundun* drum is probably the most complex drum in the world. It cannot only reproduce all speech tones, but also the glides. Its wooden body is shaped like an hourglass and the two membranes at each end are connected with leather thongs. The drummer presses these to heighten the pitch of the drum, and the average musician can produce a range of an octave. Thus, the famous Yoruba talking drum does not operate on a code system, but is simply an accurate imitation of speech melody and rhythm. A single phrase can mean a number of different things, but in context the drum talk is clear to any educated Yoruba – a Yoruba educated in his own culture, that is. Few secondary school leavers nowadays will be able to follow when the drummers recite the *oriki* (invocations) of a line of some forty odd kings, from the founder of the city right down to the living personification of the divine ruler.

Since Yoruba was not a written language, all poetry was necessarily *performance* poetry. Even an exact version written down in Yoruba could not reproduce the experience of a live performance.

Ayansola of Oshogbo was the most powerful drummer I have ever heard. His articulation was so strong, his construction of the sound patterns so firm, that people said that he was drumming "stone sculptures". On more than one occasion I have seen children fall into trance when dancing to his music – even during a social rather than a religious occasion!

Ayandokun of Iragbiji on the other hand was a much more lyrical perfomer: his whole performance was much gentler, more seductive and floating.

The drum's most sacred use is a recitation of royal or divine *oriki*. It also has many other uses, the main one being the flattery of celebrants or dancers or passers-by, who are expected to dip their hands in their pockets when they hear their ancestors named and place a coin or a note on the drummer's forehead in appreciation. The drummer is trained early to live off others in this way: in some drummers' families it is common that when a male child is born, water is *borrowed* from a neighbour to wash him.

An amusing example of the different interpretations one could put on a drummer's isolated phrase is the signal of the Nigerian Broadcasting Service (NBS). An illiterate drummer was asked to say: "This is the Nigerian Broadcasting Service." The drummer listened to this phrase, which was pronounced in English by a Nigerian speaker and he produced the following tone sequence, which became NBS's signature tune:

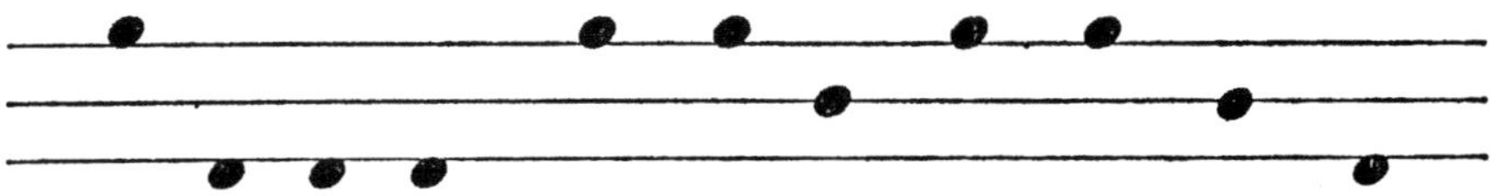

Now, of course, the average person did not know the origin of the phrase and, looking for a meaning, he came up with the following:

> *B́ólúbàdàn bá kú, tanì ó joyè*
> When the chief of Ibadan dies, who will be his successor?

Other versions were:

> *ojẹ̀gẹ̀dẹ̀ dudu, inú nta bọ̀n ùn*
> He eats black banana, then he has belly trouble.

> *kò sólòsì níbí, lo sílé kejì*
> No one is poor here, go to the next house.

The only way to render Yoruba poetry properly in English would probably be to set it to music. Even then, one would not be able to give the effect of words like:

òyányànyán	a sexy bitch
abìdírètérèté	owner of a bare bottom
jìngìndìríngín	pleasant

Nor could one, in a language that has twenty-one vowel sounds, produce a line like:

> *olójú orógbó ó ó*
> he who has eyes like bitter kola nuts

or:

> *ojumọ mọ́, nkò gbo poro poro odó,*
> *ọ̀ganjọ́ gàn, nkọ̀ gbọ́ wọ̀sọ̀ wọ̀sọ̀ kọ̀nkọ̀sọ̀.*
>
> I did not hear the sound of mortar in the morning,
> neither did I hear that of the sieve at dusk.

E.L Lasebikan[1] has argued that in Yoruba poetry, tone pattern takes the place of metre. He says that many Yoruba poems are arranged in such a way that the tones on the last syllables form a repetitive pattern. This is one of the examples he cites:

Ẹni a ní ó fẹ́'ni l'oju, o
fata sẹnu; (mid)
Ẹni a bá fẹhin ti k'a mu didun ọsàn (low)
kikan ni unfun 'ni mu; (mid)
Ẹni a ba f'inu hàn (low)
o kúkú j'alarôkiri eni. (mid)

The one we asked to blow out a speck from the eye
put pepper in his mouth
The person we could have counted on to give us sweet oranges
came with sour ones
And the one who should have been our confidant
is the one spreading gossip and rumours in the streets.

But others have pointed out that most poems show no such regularity in tone pattern, and in any case, to be convinced that tone pattern takes the place of metre one would have to be shown repetition of whole phrases or sequences. The idea that the last syllable alone should be significant was probably suggested to Lasebikan by the European device of rhyme.

Rhyme itself is absent from Yoruba poetry, but there is alliteration and particularly vowel harmony. As we have seen, it is possible to have whole lines that make use of only one vowel. Other poetic devices are the play with tones (of which examples have been given earlier), sound images like *oparara,* 'hand clapping'; *wẹ̀rìwẹ̀rì*, 'chuckle'; *sara-sara-sara*, 'blood splashing from a knife wound'; *tin tin*, 'small'; *rabata*, 'large'. The sound of a woman walking with short steps is given as *kó kò kó kò kó*, whereas a man's heavy stride is *kò kà kò kà*. Yoruba poetry uses the same figures of speech as poetry in European languages. Imagery and metaphor, simile, hyperbole, repetitions and refrains are some of the elements that translation can, in fact, do justice to.

Some previous translations have shown that Yoruba verse does not fit into any regular metre. The rhythm of Yoruba poetry has never been properly

---

[1] E.L. Lasebikan: "The tonal structure in Yoruba poetry", in: *Présence Africaine* 8-10 (1957).

analysed, but it is clearly a free and irregular rhythm. S.A. Babalola[2] explains that a Yoruba rhythm unit is really a "sense group spoken in one breath". Stress in Yoruba according to him is not inherent in particular words, but is a "function of the rhythm unit". He then proceeds to establish the following 'rules':

1) Every rhythm unit must have one stressed syllable;
2) Rhythm units with more than one stress are rare;
3) Rhythm segments are not necessarily equal in syllabic length;
4) A line can have one, two, three, four or five rhythm sections;
5) A rhythm section has one stress to anything from one to ten unstressed syllables;
6) The stresses can occur in any position in the rhythm section.

I analysed one of the poems he quotes as an example and it provides the following pattern of rhythm sections and stresses:

no. of syllables:	2	position of stress:	1st syllable
	5		4th
	3		2nd
	8		7th
	6		4th
	5		2nd
	5		2nd
	7		6th
	6		4th
	5		5th
	8		1st

It seems a complicated way of saying that Yoruba has no metre comparable to European poetic systems. This is to be expected, because there is a negligible difference between short and long vowels or between stressed and unstressed syllables. A Yoruba syllable that carries as little stress as the second syllable of the English word 'father' is simply inconceivable, because such a syllable could not carry the tone that is essential to the meaning of the word. A proper examination of Yoruba poetic rhythm would be a job for a musicologist. Most Yoruba poetry is chanted or sung, much is accompanied by drumming; the talking drum often plays poetry *across* a dance rhythm. An investigation like Babalola's cannot give us the full picture, because he counts only the syllables and not the pauses.

---

[2] S.A. Babalola: *The Content and Form of Yoruba Ijala.* Oxford: Clarendon Press 1966.

But the translator's problems and frustrations are by no means over when he has resigned himself to the fact that he cannot render the music of Yoruba poetry, nor its perpetual play on tone patterns, vowel harmonies and sound pictures, and that his rhythm can only be a remote approximation of the original. Yoruba is a *learned* language, and as such, full of allusions which remain meaningless to the reader who was brought up outside the culture. The Yoruba phrase *ọba kò so* (one of the *oriki* of the Yoruba thunder god Shango) literally means 'the king did not hang himself', which is meaningless unless one knows that Shango, the king of Oyo, *did* hang himself because he was disappointed with his rebellious subjects, that he ascended to heaven, and that his friends worshipped him after his death and defiantly made everybody pronounce the phrase: *ọba kò so*.

A Yoruba, on hearing the words 'we know whom we love...' will immediately complete the phrase in his mind: '...but we do not know who loves us'. Often the translation must complete such phrases if the reader is not to be left completely puzzled. The refrain 'the worm is dancing...' in a song about Shango implies the proverb: 'the worm is dancing, but that is merely the way it walks'. Which in turn implies the meaning: you think Shango is angry with *you*, but in fact that is just his manner of talking. S.A. Babalola quotes an excellent example of mythical (or historical) allusion:

> *labalábá kan 'mi età, ó fò rakinrakin*
> the butterfly came upon the civet cat's excrement and flew up to a great height

Babalola explains the allusion as follows: "This sentence is chanted as part of the salute to Ogun, and it is an allusion to a story which runs thus: one day, during his wanderings in his lifetime, Ogun reached a town that he had never visited before. At the town gate the tall gatekeeper on duty denied him entry. Ogun was immediately infuriated and decided to teach the gatekeeper a lesson. Therefore, he walked back a little and then executed a magnificent jump, landing on the shoulders of the standing gatekeeper. Then Ogun sat astride the man's neck and pressed down vigorously on him. The manner in which Ogun almost literally flew up to sit on the gatekeeper's shoulders resembled the manner in which butterflies, on finding a civet cat's faeces, are said to fly up for joy first of all, before they settle down for a feast."

And again, to understand Shango's *oriki* 'huge sacrifice, too heavy for the vulture', we must know about the story that tells of a fight between Heaven and Earth. Heaven and Earth went hunting together and caught only one rat between them. They quarrelled over who should have the rat and in the end, they both went home angry. Then Heaven refused to send rain and there was famine on earth. Finally the 401 gods came together and persuaded Earth to beg forgiveness from Heaven. A sacrifice was prepared, but no one wanted to carry it to Heaven. In the end, the vulture was persuaded to go, but the road to Heaven was long and the sacrifice heavy; that is why he has a bald patch on his head.

In translating poetry from a very different culture, the problem often is that we have to suffocate the actual text in an entanglement of notes. A phrase like 'huge sacrifice, too heavy for the vulture' does have some direct appeal, of course, even without the story behind it: the phrase is unusual enough to stimulate our imagination. However, when it comes to a poem like this, we need a commentary:

> God never did well when he failed to create me a woman:
> I would dance *tadireke*,
> I would open my wrapper and regard my new god
> who gives birth on the ground and who kills to eat.

To make sense of this hunters' poem we must know that *tadireke* is a popular dance in which a woman bends down and, while her head is hung low, her bottom wriggles up in the air and she opens her wrapper gracefully and reties it. The 'new god' refers, of course, to the vagina, and 'kills to eat' is an allusion to the hunters' charm, *magun*, against adultery. It is supposed to kill any man who sleeps with a hunter's wife.

Occasionally problems of context and unfamiliar reference can be solved by actually enlarging the text of the translation –

> *olójú orógbó ó*
> *ẹlẹ́kẹ̀ obì o ò*

– another description of Shango, means literally:

> eyes like bitter kola nut
> cheeks like red kola nut!

but I have rendered this:

> eyes white like bitter kola nut
> cheeks round like red kola nut

because the Yoruba is familiar with these nuts, which he handles daily, and the whiteness and roundness are implied meanings.

Overall, the problem of notes can only be solved by careful selection. A scholarly translation of Yoruba texts, whose purpose is to throw light on the culture of the Yoruba, will tend to include everything, however untranslatable. A literary translation, whose main purpose is to try to convey the feeling and mood of Yoruba poetry to the English reader, will have to weed out material that is of purely ethnographic interest. It will have to provide a selection that is limited to what is most successfully transposed into English.

The Yoruba oracle, for example, consists of a vast body of ritual verse. This contains some of the finest poetry in the Yoruba language, but it is top-heavy with prescriptions for sacrifices, long and somewhat repetitive lists running something like this: two hundred snails, two chickens, two goats, two pots of palm oil and two shillings and six pence... Even these recipes can sound poetic when they are chanted in the correct tone and accompanied by the heavy sound of *gbedu* drums during a ceremony that lasts all night by the flickering light of sixteen oil-lamps. However, translated into English and transposed into cold print, they are as irritatingly dull as the "And Abraham begat Isaac and Isaac begat..." chapters of the Bible.

Two other qualities of the Yoruba language frustrate the translator. One is its capacity for compiling phrases into monster nouns or adjectives like:

erin abìkúnlẹ̀pelemọmọ	huge as a hill even when kneeling
ọtamọkunkunbioyin	he who keeps stinging like a swarm of bees

Even in German (which can pride itself on words like *Oberbahnhofsvorsteher*), it would be difficult to attempt these poetic tongue twisters. In English, the feeble device of joining a number of words with hyphens totally fails to convey the pleasure with which the Yoruba hunter or praise-singer spits out such a mouthful.

Even more frustrating is the Yoruba method of interpreting familiar words to prove a particular point. In English words like 'mother' or 'wife' are basic words. No etymologist would attempt to find other words or concepts from which they could have been derived. The Yoruba oracle, however, interprets *iyawó*, 'wife', to mean 'punishment in the town of Iwo' and alleges that the word is composed of *ìyà*, 'punishment', and Iwo. One of the ritual stories of the oracle tells us how Orunmila, the god of the oracle, went to prison in Iwo for an alleged offence, but when it was discovered that he was innocent the king gave him a wife in recompense. Used in the right context, therefore, the word *iyawó* can have an implied meaning of 'recompense for suffering', but any translation would automatically lose such overtones.

The delight Yorubas take in interpreting words and the fantastic derivations they construct have the effect of keeping the words alive and always slightly ambivalent. Certainly, it prevents words from becoming clichés. When asking a number of friends what they thought of the above piece of etymology, they immediately produced rival interpretations. T.S. Sowande suggested that *iyá*, 'mother', is someone who draws a picture and *iyawómi*, 'my wife', is someone who draws my picture (*yá*, 'to draw'; *aworan*, 'picture'). However, Bakare Gbadamosi[3] suggested that *iyá* means: 'from where we branch' (the verb *yá* also means 'to branch').

E.B. Idowu, professor of Religious Studies at the University of Ibadan, gives five different interpretations of the word *Olódùmarè*, God:[4]

olodu ọmọ ere	supreme one, offspring of the boa
olodu ma re	supreme one who remains constant
olodu mọ are	supreme one who wears the crown
olodu kari	the perfect one
olodumare	the one to whom I must return

All five added together, he believes, prove that the Yoruba concept of the high god was not very different from the Christian one. Of course, Rev. Samuel Johnson in his *The History of the Yorubas*[5] has quite a different idea. *Olodumare* to him means: *Olodu*, 'father of the Odu' (that is Oduduwa, the ancestor of the Yoruba race); *ma rè*, 'cannot go beyond', that is, the Almighty.

This play with words and meanings becomes hot stuff when it concerns the names of towns and places. The town of Ilobu is only one and a half miles from Ifon. Although Ifon appears to be a much older town, Ilobu is now much bigger and more important. The King of Ilobu therefore is anxious to

---

[3] Verbal communication.

[4] E.B. Idowu: *Olodumare*. London 1962.

[5] Rev. Samuel Johnson: *The History of the Yorubas*. London: Routledge 1921.

forget the fact that his ancestors settled on a piece of land provided by the King of Ifon. The common interpretation of the name Ilobu is *ìlú owu*, 'cotton town'. This interpretation supports the legend that the King of Ilobu was a hunter, who rendered some service to the King of Ifon, who gave him a daughter for wife and told him to build his house on one of the king's cotton-fields. This interpretation is inconvenient to the King of Ilobu, who is anxious that his people should stop paying land dues (*isakole*) to Ifon. His interpretation, therefore, is *ìlú obu*, 'town of rock salt'. According to him, his people could not get salt when they first came to settle on that spot and had to resort to rock salt.

Even more spectacular are the interpretations of the title *Ooni*, the sacred King of Ife. Dr Lucas believes that *Ooni* simply means 'crocodile', and this indicates that the title is a religious title (the crocodile is sacred in Ife). The Ife people themselves interpret the title as meaning 'owner of the land' (contracted from *oonile*), whereas Johnson, the Yoruba historian, suggests that *Ooni* is contacted from *ọmọ oluwọ ni*, which means 'son of a sacrificial victim'. This interpretation is offered in support of the claim by the rival city of Oyo that the King of Ife is a spiritual head, not a political one. It also supports a myth that tries to explain the precarious balance of power between the two towns, at the same time hiding certain historical facts. Most historians and anthropologists accept as fact today that Ife is a much older city, that the Oyos represent a much later wave of immigration and that they reduced the dominant position of Ife as a political power. Certain recognition had to be given to the King of Ife, however, as the original owner of the land who alone knew how to deal with the spirits of the land. The Ife gods were admitted into the Oyo pantheon and through them the *Ooni*, though deprived of political power, continued to exercise considerable influence. The Oyos invented a myth according to which Oranmiyan, the founder of their city, was in fact a King of Ife, and the *Ooni* was the son of a woman who was supposed to be sacrificed to Obatala, the god of creation, but was spared when found pregnant. The child grew up to become the King's favourite priest. One day Oranmiyan set out on a military campaign. He left the *Ooni* in charge of the shrines and the city, taking all his warriors and chiefs with him. The campaign proved a failure (he was prevented from crossing the Niger as he had intended) and he was ashamed to return without a victory to his credit. Therefore, he founded a new city, Oyo. To be crowned, however, he had to send for the ritual objects from Ife and since then every *Ooni* has to play an important part in the coronation of the King of Oyo (almost like the Pope crowning the German emperors). So the fantastic interpretation of *Ooni* as *ọmọ oluwọ ni* enables the Oyos to disguise the historical fact of conquest, lay a fictitious claim to original ownership of the land, explain their seniority over Ife, and at the same time acknowledge their dependency on Ife in spiritual matters. What looks like phoney philology is, in fact, good politics.

With so much lost in translation there is still a great deal that survives. The imagery of Yoruba poetry can be staggering: God sits in the sky like a swarm of bees; death drops *to, to, to* like indigo from a cloth that is being dyed; the god of fate hits a stone until it bleeds when angry; the elephant tears a man like a rag and hangs him up in a tree.

Yoruba humour stops at nothing: the divine warrior king 'swallows a hero every time he opens his mouth'. The thunder god eats so much pounded yam that he begins to look like a pregnant woman. There is playful abuse: the forest god Erinle is accused of being a ragged lice-ridden god.

The Yorubas like to call a spade a spade and there are no really dirty words. The little song with which girls drive away boys from their game –

> Penis penis plays by himself.
> Vagina vagina plays by herself.
> We shall not play with somebody
> who has sixteen testicles

– was given to me by a six year old girl. Children's riddles define the vagina alternatively as 'a small bearded god, whom we must worship kneeling down' and 'a little bush becomes a court case'. Yoruba humour is baroque and earthy, never vicious. It is playful banter that knows about the weaknesses of human beings ('the Muslim says he does not eat monkeys; when Salawu is hungry he eats a baboon!'), but it never despises them.

Poetry comes more naturally to the Yoruba than prose. When a child is born, it is given three kinds of names. The name which the child 'has brought from heaven' is suggested by circumstances of birth: *Ọmọpẹ*, 'the child is late'; *Ajayi*, 'born face-downwards'; *Ojo*, 'born with the navel cord around his neck'; *Abiọna*, 'born by the wayside'; and so on. To this will be added the *abisọ*, the name of the parents' choice: *Ayọdele*, 'joy has entered the house'; *Ogundalenu*, 'our home was devastated by war'; *Adegbitẹ*, 'the crown demands a throne'; *Adepọju*, 'the coming of children has become too much'. The third name is the *oriki*, which is the praise name, the descriptive name, the pet name, and the poetic name. One's *oriki* may express some hope or feeling of the parents: *Alakẹ́*, 'one to be petted if she survives'; *Akunyun*, 'one who rushes about'; *Ajani*, 'one who conquers after a struggle', etc. But it is when the person grows up, particularly when he is a distinguished person, that the drummers will invent more and more names to build up his public image. A king would have dozens of such *oriki*, some inherited from his ancestors and many specifically his own. In Ede, the Timi collected the *oriki* of the last fifteen rulers. These reveal an essentially different set of *oriki* for each Timi, with the odd one repeated here and there.

The *oriki* is the basic form of Yoruba poetry. Nothing is exempt from it: kings, gods, towns, animals, and plants. 'The young bride who rubbed her body with camwood' is one of the *oriki* of cassava; 'cassava and maize are your poor relations' is one of the *oriki* of the yam. The *oriki* of Europeans is 'a pair of shorts that can worry a large embroidered gown'. *Oriki* are frequently recited on the drum. They are sung by the *akewi*, the praise-singers at a king's court. The *oriki* of a god would be sung by his worshippers; that of an animal or plant by hunters.

Apart from the *oriki*, the most important forms of Yoruba poetry are the *ijala*, the *iwi*, the *odu* and *rara*. *Ijala* is the poetry of hunters. It is chanted usually during the festivals of the god Ogun, the god of iron who is worshipped by all those who use iron – hunters, warriors and circumcision experts. Their poetry talks about animals of the bush and about plants. They recite the *oriki* of Ogun and the deeds of important hunters. Some *Ijala* are collections of random remarks and jokes.

Iwi is the poetry of the *Egungun* masqueraders, who are the manifestations of ancestors. They know the invocations of towns and lineages. There are other masqueraders, the *Agbegijo* or *Alarinjo*, who are itinerant entertainers whose performances include skits on Hausamen, Europeans, policemen and prostitutes. Their songs include comments on human weaknesses like greed and laziness.

Odu Ifa is the poetry of the Yoruba oracle. The Yoruba diviner, or *babalawo* ('father of secrets') has an elaborate system of divination by which he arrives at a particular *odu* in the Ifa corpus of poetry. There are sixteen *odu*, each of which is again subdivided into sixteen subsections, making 256 in all. Each of the 256 smaller *odu* consists of a poem or song, a story, and a prescription for sacrifice.

Rara is, as it were, lay poetry, in contrast to the highly specialized forms like *iwi*, *ijala* and *odu*. A bride proceeding to her husband's house, surrounded by all her relatives and friends, sings in praise of her mother, or in anticipation of the life that awaits her in the new home.

Different forms of Yoruba poetry are distinguished by the style of singing or chanting. Occasionally the subject matter is similar or overlapping. The enunciation differs, however. Though Yoruba song has to follow the basic tone-pattern of speech, the intervals can be heightened or reduced. The word *àpáta* (rock) cannot be sung

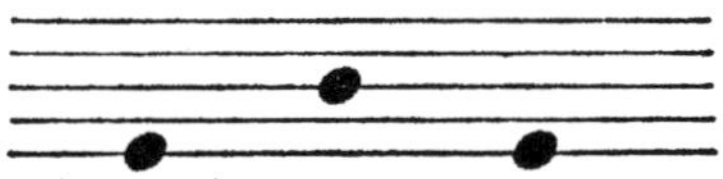

or else it would be understood to mean 'shield'. However, any of the following three versions would still be understood as 'rock':

Again, the singer can suddenly raise or drop the entire pitch of his singing. All this is possible, as long as the relationships of tones *within* a word remain correct. Anybody familiar with Yoruba poetry can identify a hunter, a masquerader or an Ifa priest chanting, merely by listening to the style of chanting or singing, and quite regardless of the words he is using.

In translation, these very important distinctions are necessarily lost.

Some authors have tried to translate Yoruba poetry into English verse. S.A. Babalola, who pioneered the study of the *ijala*, Yoruba hunters' poetry, rendered it in blank verse. But the alien rhythm put the poems into a kind of straight jacket and associations with English blank verse produced strangely stilted lines, like "with arrogance unparalleled he spoke", "and points towards with all his fingers ten", or "with reverent homage and appropriate rites". I have therefore preferred to be less ambitious. Accepting the fact that many elements of Yoruba poetry are simply untranslatable, I feel that a simple rendering can convey the vitality, the humour, the startling imagery and the wisdom of Yoruba poetry.

To do full justice to it we must recreate it as performance poetry. Using a foreign language one could not attempt to copy it, but one can turn it into a new art form, which hopefully will have a similar spiritual energy and power. Wole Soyinka has in fact done so in an extraordinary CD called "Wole Soyinka reads Yoruba poetry with Okuta Percussion", which was published by Migila in 1994.

Ulli Beier

Sydney 2002

THE ORIGIN OF THIS BOOK

I first experienced Yoruba poetry fifty years ago. In the summer of 1951 I visited Timi Laoye I, the ruler of the Yoruba kingdom of Ede. We were discussing the possibility of introducing university adult education classes to Ede, when a group of drummers entered the courtyard, reciting the Timi's *oriki*. I was still very new in the country, but I could enjoy the performance as pure music. While the ensemble played a relaxed dance rhythm, the leader – so it seemed to me then – was improvising freely across it. But the Timi explained that he was in fact reciting poetry and he translated the odd phrase for me:

> Nobody can prevent the monkey
> from sitting on the branch of a tree.

I was immediately captivated: in what other culture could you praise a king by comparing him to a monkey? And yet: what perfect metaphor to suggest that the Timi was secure on his throne!

> Son of a king who owned elephants!
> You are beautiful like young raffia
> on top of a palm tree.

Every line was surprising – nothing seemed familiar at all.

When I started my adult education classes in English literature in Ede, the Timi attended my weekly classes for a whole year because he wanted to encourage his towns people. I felt embarrassed because what he taught me about Yoruba poetry and philosophy was so much more fascinating and relevant than what I could tell him about English literature.

I moved to Ede to be close to him, and for several years I saw him almost daily. He taught me about the history of his town, invited me to attend all the big festivals of the Yoruba *orisha* and shared his wisdom and his knowledge with me. My enthusiasm seemed to stimulate his own passion for his culture: he picked up the little talking drum again, which he had played as a child, and he even took lessons from his head drummer. He published articles on Yoruba drums and lectured on drum poetry, not only in Nigeria but in Germany, the US and even Rhodesia.

In 1957 I moved to Oshogbo, a Yoruba town just fifteen kilometres from Ede. There I found two new friends, who helped me to pursue my interest in Yoruba poetry. Both had only received a primary school education, but they were exceptionally gifted and imaginative people. Bakare Gbadamosi was about twenty-five years old. He was unemployed and at a loose end. I liked his boisterous sense of humour, his curiosity and his boundless energy. Six years of primary education had not succeeded to alienate him from his culture. He had a profound knowledge of 'deep' Yoruba and could 'read' the talking drum's poetry. He introduced me to his relatives: priests of the river goddess Oya and members of the hunters' guild. We began to collect some of their poetry and tried to make translations that worked as English poetry rather than being anthropological records. We attended festivals in Ede, Ilobu, Ifon, Okuku and further afield, collecting oracle verses, the chants of masqueraders and the invocations of the gods. We collected poetry from the children in our own compound in Oshogbo. Our close association lasted until I left Nigeria in December 1966.

Duro Ladipo was the son of a catechist in the Anglican Church of Oshogbo, and he had grown up in an environment that was severely prejudiced against 'pagan' Yoruba traditions. But he was far too intelligent to accept such narrow-minded attitudes. In 1961 he shocked his father and the church elders when he performed his "Easter Cantata" in All Saints Church to the accompaniment of Yoruba talking drums. When he was banned from performing his music in the church, he decided to start a theatre company. His first play was a disappointment. In the tradition of Yoruba popular theatre of the time he wrote a slapstick comedy. The action was underlined by percussionists playing simple rhythms on bongos and congas. I gave him a copy of the Reverend Johnson's *The History of the Yorubas*. Because of the mission education he had received, he had not even heard of it. Now he immersed himself in this unique source material and became totally fascinated! He visited the Timi of Ede and other Yoruba rulers, talked to Yoruba priests, hunters and musicians to collect Yoruba history, myths and poetry. He began to write tragedies, making full use of the traditional Yoruba drum ensembles: the *dundun*, *bata* and *igbin*. Timi Laoye travelled to Oshogbo once a week to train some of the cast as performers on the talking drum. The actors and musicians had little Western education, if any. They were highly motivated and some of them contributed dances, incantations or songs to the plays. Duro never wrote these plays down. The cast learned the songs by heart, but much of the dialogue was improvised. No two performances were ever alike.

Before taking his company abroad for the first time – he had been invited to perform *Oba Koso* in Berlin in 1964 – we found it necessary to tighten up the play and produce a more predictable performance, based on a written text. Examining his play closely, Duro discovered that the language was inconsistent. There were beautiful poetic passages, making use of ancient Yoruba poetry like the final chorus, which celebrates the immortality of the deceased king:

> Fire in your eyes,
> fire in your mouth,
> fire on the roofs!
> The kite was lost in the sky
> and returned to its nest.
> The banana was cut down
> but bears new fruit.
> Two hundred glowing embers
> must bow down to the fire.
> Two hundred warriors
> must bow down to death.
> Two hundred stars
> must worship the sun!

But these were interspersed with very colloquial modern Yoruba. Duro tried to achieve more uniformity in the tone of his play. We spent several weeks producing an English text, which he then translated back into Yoruba. We both enjoyed this activity so much that we proceeded to work on two more plays together. The English versions of *Oba Koso*, *Oba Moro* and *Oba Waja* were published by Mbari in 1964.

Having spent a couple of months working with Duro on the English versions of his plays, I was in such high spirits and had got into such a rhythm that I could not resist the temptation of writing some plays for the Duro Ladipo Theatre myself. I wrote three plays. *Everyman* was based on a modern German play[6], but transposed into a Yoruba cultural setting; *The Imprisonment of Obatala* was based on an ancient Yoruba myth, and *Woyengi* was adapted from an Ijaw creation story. Duro translated them into Yoruba and they became part of his repertoire. Heinemann published the original English versions in 1966, but because I had drawn so heavily on Yoruba poetry and because I owed so much to Duro Ladipo, Bakare

---

6 Hugo von Hofmannsthal's *Jedermann*, which is the highlight of the annual Salzburg festival. Duro's Yoruba translation of *Everyman* was performed in Salzburg in 1965.

Gbadamosi and Timi Laoye, I was reluctant to put my name to it. My pseudonym, Ijimere, was of course a joke: Ijimere is my favourite monkey. Ironically it became my best-selling publication!

The exuberant spirit of Duro Ladipo also inspired members of his cast to become authors. Tijani Mayakiri published a book on the verses of the Ifa oracle. Muraina Oyelami, who became a drummer with an international reputation, published the first teaching manuals on the drum poetry of the *dundun* and the *bata* ensembles. Ademola Onibonokuta made a collection of magic formulas, which he had learned from his old father who was a traditional herbalist. Sixteen of the formulas are published in this book in English adaptations which we produced together.

These Yoruba friends helped me to explore the wonderful world of Yoruba poetry. For several decades our lives were closely interwoven. This book is one of many publications that emerged from our close association. The Timi, Bakare and Duro have all departed before me, but the poetry they introduced me to is still as fresh as ever. Its humour is still potent and its wisdom is still relevant. These poems still "amuse, amaze, astonish and enchant"[7].

---

[7] The quotation is from Milan Kundera, who demands these four qualities from the novel.

GODS[1]

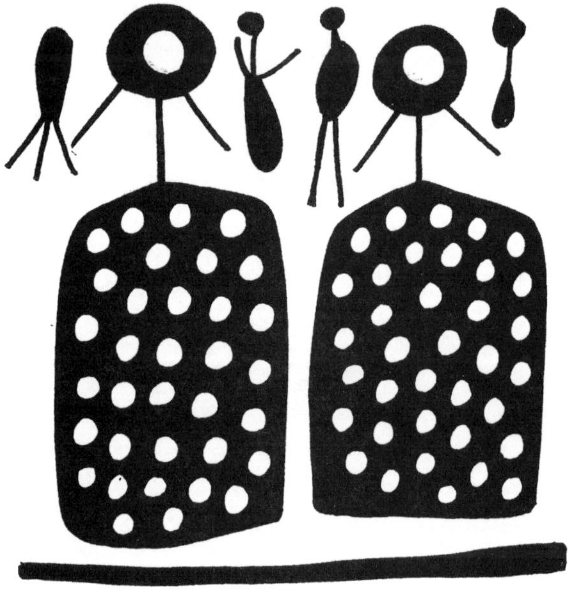

ESHU[2]

Eshu turns right into wrong, wrong into right.
When he is angry, he hits a stone until it bleeds.
When he is angry, he sits on the skin of an ant.
When he is angry, he weeps tears of blood.
Eshu slept in the house –
but the house was too small for him.
Eshu slept on the verandah –
but the verandah was too small for him.
Eshu slept in a nut –
at last he could stretch himself.
Eshu walked through the groundnut farm,
the tuft of his hair was just visible.
If it had not been for his huge size,
he would not be visible at all.
Lying down, his head hits the roof.
Standing up, he cannot look into the cooking pot.
He throws a stone today
and kills a bird yesterday.

OBATALA[3]

He is patient.
He is silent.
Without anger he pronounces his judgement.
He is distant,
but his eye rests on the town.
He kills the initiate
and rouses him to new life.
He is playful like death,
he carries the child away.
He rides the hunchback,
he spreads out his arms,
the right and the left.
He stands by his children,
he lets them succeed.
He makes them laugh –
and they laugh.
You, father of laughter,
your eye is laughing.
Immense granary of the sky.
Old man with the strength of youth,
you rest in the sky like a swarm of bees.
The rich owe their riches to you.
The poor owe their poverty to you.
You take from the rich and give to the poor.
Take then from the rich and give to me.
Obatala,
you turn blood into children,
come and create the child in my own belly.
I own but a single cloth to dye with indigo.
I own but a single headtie to dye with camwood.
But I know:
you have twenty or thirty children waiting for me,
whom I shall bear!

ODUDUWA[4]

He is spreading fear on the roads
and terror in the compounds,
but he will not let me die of hunger.
He will drive my creditor away from my threshold,
he will thrust my enemy's sword
into his own intestines.

He wakes in the morning,
he arises radiantly,
he creates,
he does not destroy.

He fights the fire and conquers fire.
He fights the sun and conquers the sun.
With a calabash he threatens the water,
the calabash cannot break the surface of the water,
he sprinkles earth over the water.
Creator of land,
founder of cities!

Wild battle in heaven,
divine quarrel among brothers,
God's palace resounds with battle cries.
Oduduwa washes the big pot in the morning,
he washes it clean,
he prepares it for war.

He is the husband,
he is the wife.
Warm like the sun,
cool like the harmattan.
He builds a house of parrot's feathers,
a wall of darkness
that reaches into the sky.

OSHUMARE[5]

Oshumare
rests above the clouds,
his long arm
stretches across the face of the sky,
he lets the rain fall onto the earth,
he lets the yam grow in the soil.

Oshumare
fetches the coral from the sea,
he breaks the red carnelian from the rock
and digs the blue segi out of the ground.

The father
who enters our courtyard
and makes our children grow,
who grants us long life
and brings us success.

Huge like the sky,
owner of innumerable kola nuts!
Eat only one –
and you will be satisfied!

He enters the bush
growling like rain,
he enters the forest
sparkling like the sun.
Husband of Ijoko,
the indigo forest has no thorns,
husband of Ijoko,
he watches the world with his black eye.

YEMOJA[6]

Queen from the depth of the ocean,
ruler of the world.
When others prostrate before the king
she remains seated.
Healing mother,
old magician,
ruler of the seas!

Whirlpool of the ocean,
fighting arena for wind and waves,
Tidal wave!
When she is angry
she swallows bridges!

Queen
Mother whose breasts weep tears,
mother with bearded vagina,
virgin
whose vagina is frigid
like dry yams.

Flutist
whose melody delights us at dawn,
flutist
whose lament echoes in the palace.

Black river
red river
queen
who rises from the waves
splendid like the rainbow
and gently
very gently
she gathers her people around her.

SHONPONA[7]

Shonpona spare me!
When we eat maize, we spare the leaf,
when we eat yam, we spare the knife.
Is the tree not forgiven because it is gnarled?
Is the albino not forgiven because the creator made him so?
Shonpona, forgive me,
I am walking in darkness,
spare me,
and let me walk in the sun too.
Let me not meet the heavenly tormentor,
let my children not meet him either!
Your home is near the river,
jingling horseman, fast traveller,
who settles his quarrels with a spear.
The road is clouded in dust,
when you pursue your enemy.
Your home is by the river.
I cannot walk the sea or the lagoon,
let me sail upon Elentere river
until I reach the wide river Niger.
Shonpona,
I have leaves and flowers to heal,
and a rough cloth to carry my child.
I use banana fibres to carry my child to the market.
Who will find me the soft cotton?
Who will bring me the honeycomb?
Soft cotton is brought to the market
and becomes plentiful.
But the honeycomb becomes dear.
The dead are difficult to bury!
Many people are asleep, who will never wake up!

Shonpona, please wake me in my own room,
and let my child wake up too.

Shonpona, it is not good of you not to spare me!
But if you want to carry my load,
let me follow you to your home by the river.
Jingling horseman in a cloud of dust,
carry me to your home in the bush,
heavenly tormentor,
hold me, hold me in your arm.

SHANGO[8]

Huge sacrifice,
too heavy for the vulture,
it trembles under your weight.
Huge morsel,
we cannot digest you.
If anyone tried to swallow you –
you would be out through his anus
like lightning!
Your eyes are white like bitter kola nut.
Your cheeks are round like red kola nut.
Fire-spitting masquerader,
you frighten the big cat.
Invulnerable one:
who can behead a fly?
who can crush a tortoise?
who can swallow a hedgehog?
You die in the market
and wake up in the house.
Like the kite that was lost in the sky
you return to your nest.
Like the banana tree that was cut
you ripen with new fruit.
Fire in the eye, fire in the mouth, fire on the roof,
you ride fire like a horse!

Shango is the death that drips *to, to, to,*
like indigo dye dripping from a cloth.
Shango is the death that kills money with a big stick.
He is the lightning flash
wrapped in a cloak of death.
He is the leopard who kills the sheep
and bathes in its blood.

Shango strikes the stupid man,
he wrinkles his nose and the liar runs away.
Even when he does not fight we fear him.
But when war gleams in his eye,
enemies and worshippers run alike.
He walks alone,
but he enters the town like a swarm of locusts.
Crabs' feet are confusion.
The parrot's feet are crooked.
Shango went to Ibadan
and arrived in Ilorin.
The king who knows today and tomorrow.
The one who turns a bad head into a good one.
Who gives a child to the white haired woman,
the lover who buys the vagina on credit –
and asks the chief to pay the bride price.
The god who imparts his beauty
to the women with whom he sleeps.
He takes his neighbour's roof
and covers his own head.
He lends money and does not ask for it back.
If you do not offer him a seat
he will sit on top of your nose.
If you do not share your maize gruel with him
he will slip under your finger nail
and take his share.
Shango does as he pleases.
If he likes, he can make maize porridge from bananas.
If he likes, he can wear a ragged cloth like a widow.
He kneels down, like a collector of vegetables.
Shango does not collect vegetables.
He is only looking for the head of the farmer.
The farmer was deceived.
He went to the farm, only to meet his death.

OYA[9]

Dark forest
dark secret
deadly wind!
Fire is your baggage!
Consort of the red husband,
wife of thunder, who rules the world,
like Shango you confront death without fear.

There is uproar in heaven!
You hurl the axe through the clouds,
you set fire to the sky,
you smash the calabashes
and spill the palm wine,
you uproot the trees,
you carry away roofs,
you tear the liar's intestines from his belly
and push his head into the sand!

Oya! Tornado!
Delicate feet painted with camwood –
you punish the thief with blindness,
you are the only one
who can seize the buffalo by his horns.
You alone can fight the God of the sea
in his own ocean!
You quickly climb on the roof
and the red death
illuminates the night.
You kill quickly
like wildfire
and our farm is destroyed.

Oya,
the camwood gleams on your painted feet,
the cowrie shells sparkle on your black buttocks.

You look after your friends on earth,
you protect the child in the midst of battle,
you look after it during the night.
I beg you Oya,
carry me on your back,
don't drop me,
do not carry me upside down
with my head hanging down.
Mother,
do not walk in the sun with me,
bring me into the shade,
bring me home safely in the evening.
Gently
wife of thunder
gently.
We worship you, mother.
When the drummer beats the Apinti drum
it faces the sun.

OSHUN[10]

Brass and parrot feathers
on a velvet skin.
White cowrie shells
on black buttocks.
Her eyes sparkle in the forest,
like the sun on the river.
She is the wisdom of the forest,
she is the wisdom of the river.
Where the doctor failed
she cures with fresh water.
Where medicine is impotent
she cures with cool water.
She cures the child
and does not charge the father.
She feeds the barren woman with honey
and her dry body swells up
like a juicy palm fruit.
Oh, how sweet
is the touch of child's hand!

ERINLE[11]

The eye of god will not grow any grass.
The rock will not sprout with yam.
Like the earth, Erinle will never change.
He is the father of the child
and the father of the king.
He knows the dry places on earth,
he knows where the river flows.
He knows where the grass is rich
and where the bombax tree shades the river
and the air is cool like the harmattan.
He mixes the heads of vultures
with the heads of other birds.
The antelope cannot move,
the bush cow is spell-bound.
He is friendly with the leopard,
because he covets his spotted ear.
Erinle mends the broken pot,
Erinle mends the broken fortune,
he mends the broken head.
When the lamp is extinguished,
his eyes sparkle like fire.
Erinle, ragged god,
your cloth is full of lice.
Beggar and thief!
You refuse to pay for your beer!
You refuse to pay for your kola nuts!
Erinle, father of the child,
father of the king,
from the depth of the river
he calls us to war!

OGUN[12]

Ogun kills on the right and destroys on the right.
Ogun kills on the left and destroys on the left.
Ogun kills suddenly in the house and suddenly in the field.
Ogun kills the child with the iron with which it plays.
Ogun kills in silence.
Ogun kills the thief and the owner of stolen goods.
Ogun kills the owner of the house
and paints the hearth with his blood.

Ogun is the forest god.
He gives all his clothes to the beggars.
He gives one to the woodcock – who dyes it in indigo.
He gives one to the coucal – who dyes it in camwood.
He gives one to the cattle egret – who leaves it white.

Ogun's laughter is no joke.
His enemies scatter in all directions.
The butterflies do not have to see the leopard –
as soon as they smell his shit
they scatter in all directions!

Master of iron, chief of robbers,
you have water, but you bathe in blood.
The light shining in your face
is not easy to behold:
Ogun, with the bloody cap,
let me see the red of your eye.

Ogun is not like pounded yam:
do you think you can knead him in your hand
and eat of him until you are satisfied?
Do you think Ogun is something you can throw into your cap
and walk away with it?

Ogun is a mad god
who will ask questions after seven hundred and eighty years.
Ogun have pity on me:
whether I can reply, or whether I cannot reply:
Ogun don't ask me anything!

The lion never allows anybody to play with his cub.
Ogun will never allow his child to be punished.
Ogun do not reject me!
Does the woman who spins ever reject the spindle?
Does the woman who dyes ever reject a cloth?
Does the eye that sees ever reject a sight?
Ogun, do not reject me.

OSHOSI[13]

Great warrior,
great hunter!
Unperturbed
he rests in the farm of his enemy.

He pursues the villain,
his sparkling eyes
fill him with fear.

The sight of misfortune
does not frighten our eyes,
the greatest misfortune we suffer calmly.
The man who is being hanged
cannot suffocate in the mud,
the dead antelope
will not be shot by the hunter.

Little man with scintillating spirit,
we cannot hear his voice
but we hear his iron gong
echoing in the mountains.

The woodcock calls in the bush,
the parrot builds himself a house
of cowrie shells.
Everybody wants to have the parrot.

He is fast on the road,
fast with his arrows,
fast with his death.
Oshosi,
strong like four hundred buffaloes –
that's eight hundred horns!

AYAN AGALU[14]

Ayan Agalu, god of drummers,
I greet you in the morning.
Ayan Agalu
who speaks through the resonance of wood!
You force us to eat with a miser,
you force us to eat what we don't like to eat.
You force us to visit the sixteen most hidden corners of the market.

Ayan Agalu
treat me gently.

The gun is the pride of the hunter,
blood is the pride of the healer,
courage is the pride of the drummer.

Ayan Agalu
treat me gently.

OKE[15]

He is the rock whom people cannot eat,
he is the rock whom people cannot drink,
he is the rock who is unperturbed,
who carries all of us on his head.

He is the husband of 3000 hoes,
he is the husband of 3000 cutlasses.
They joined hands and rebelled against him
but the rock defeated them all!
Calm rock,
smooth and shiny like an anvil.
Rock whom people cannot eat or drink.

IYA MAPO[16]

Iya Mapo,
mother of mothers,
calm old mother of the earth.

On the day we came down to earth from heaven
you gave us our profession.
You provide for us
better than the market,
you provide for us
better even than the farm.

Iya Mapo does not support a lazy woman.
Iya Mapo says: "While we wake, we work."
Iya Mapo, who fills the day like rain,
who dances like the spinning top on the ground.
Iya Mapo, who lives in the depth of the earth.
Iya Mapo, who flutters around the hilltop
like a butterfly.

Iya Mapo,
before you I am completely naked.
Even if I own twenty slaves
I am completely naked.
Even if I have thirty Iwofa
I am completely naked.

Nobody can count your thousands!
You could buy up the whole
of Igbeti market!
You could help a king!

Iya Mapo,
you send your children on an errand,
you teach them how to walk with a bold heart.
Iya Mapo,
it is your face we are looking at!

KINGS & TOWNS[17]

THE ALAFIN OF OYO

Child of death,
father of all mothers,
king of all kings.
You carry the blackness of the forest
like a royal gown.
You carry the blood of your enemies
like a shining crown.
Be merciful with us,
as the silk cotton tree is merciful with the forest,
as the eagle is merciful with the birds.
The town rests in the palm of your hand,
weightless and fragile.
Do not destroy it:
our fate rests in your hand,
wield it carefully like your beaded sceptre.
The enemies who want to destroy you
will destroy themselves.
When they want to roast maize,
they will set fire to their roof.
When they want to sell water –
there will be drought.
The sieve will always be master of the chaff.
The waterlily will always float on the lake.
Child of death,
the hairs on your chest are as numerous
as the words of a talkative woman.
You grab the heads of your enemies
and push their faces into boiling water.
You lock the door in front of their noses
and keep the key in your pocket.
Child of death,
father of all mothers,
king of all kings.

THE OGOGA OF IKERRE

Two hundred needles do not make a hoe.
Two hundred stars do not make a moon.
However small the needle – the hen cannot swallow it.
The poisonous toad is laughing at the cook.
The termites are staring at the stone – without hope.
The albino keeps dying his hair,
but it will continue to grow white.
You are lonely,
like the solitary tailfeather of the okin bird.
We cannot enforce your blessing.
But how could you be angry?
A man can be angry but not a god.
Whether the moon shines or not –
you shine in the dark.
The lizard cannot impersonate a snake.
A man whose father is alive cannot be king.
The hunter thinks the monkey is not wise.
The monkey *is* wise – but he has his own logic.
You are the thorn in the elephant's foot.
You are the stone that breaks the lion's tooth.
You let the red palm oil flow
from the necks of men.
You are the husband of the black woman and of the yellow one.
You are the husband of the fat woman
who sells tobacco on the market.
You are a great dancer:
You dance even in the face of death.

THE ONIKOYI OF IKOYI

Onikoyi, the warrior who never received an arrow in his back.
Child of the waterlily, child of the squirrel.
The bird's foot shall never touch the water,
the river shall never be at rest.
Onikoyi, the warrior
who frightens death himself.
Child of the vulture perching on the baobab tree.
Child of the eagle sitting on the silk cotton tree.
Child of the hawk waiting on the camwood tree.
When the vulture flaps down
he will eat the intestines of a brave warrior.
When the eagle glides down
he will eat the liver of a brave warrior.
When the hawk pounces down
he will eat the eyes of a brave warrior.
Onikoyi loves nothing but war:
when others drink wine, he drinks blood.
When others plant yams, he is planting heads.
When others reap fruit, he is reaping dead warriors.
One day Onikoyi went out to rob.
Then a thief broke into his own house.
Onikoyi met the thief on the road.
The thief said: 'Ha – is that not Onikoyi?'
Onikoyi said: 'Ha – is that not the thief?'
They pounce on each other.
Onikoyi cuts off the thief's head.
The thief cries: 'Oshun, Shonpona, help me!'
Onikoyi replies: 'Whether you call Oshun
or whether you call Shonpona,
I am the one who cuts off the heads.
For every warrior is a bit of thief.'

THE TIMI OF EDE

Huge fellow whose body fills an anthill,
you are heavily pregnant with war.
All your body except your teeth is black.
No one can prevent the monkey
from sitting on the branch of a tree.
No one can dispute the throne with you.
No one can try to fight you.
One who shakes a tree trunk shakes himself.
We do not resist you.
The seeds of the Ayo game
do not complain of being shoved about.
You are like death
who plucks a man's eyeballs suddenly.
You are like a big ripe fruit
that falls on a child at midnight.
Fighting a battle in front
you mark out the next battlefield behind.
My Lord, please give the world some rest.
If one greets you, there is trouble;
if one does not greet you, there is also trouble.
The fire of destruction is part of your baggage
wherever you go.
You kill your opponents gently,
like cutting a calabash in two.
When the leopard kills,
its tail trails gently on the ground.
Whenever you open your mouth wide,
you swallow a hero.

IBADAN[18]

The spirit of the rock protects the town.
Ibadan, don't fight!
We must ask for permission before we enter the town,
because this is the town in which the thief is innocent
and the owner of property is guilty.
Here peace is lying exhausted on the ground
and belligerence dances on his back.
Ibadan, the town where the owner of the land
does not prosper like a stranger.
Nobody is born without some kind of disease in his body.
Riots in all the compounds are the diseases of Ibadan.
You think you have friends in Ibadan –
but they will sell your own child.
You may look at this town whichever way you like –
you will see nothing but war.

ORACLE VERSES[19]

Lies travel for twenty years and never arrive.
A liar went on a journey for six months and never arrived.
But truth says, it is better to deliver the truth and die.

I am blessing two, not one.
This was prophesied to the sealily
which reaches down into the mud,
the origin of creation.
The time of creation has come.

The sky is immense, but grows no grass.
This is what the oracle said to Obatala,
to whom the great god gave the reins of the world.
God of the Igbo[20], I stretch out my hands,
give the reins of the world to me.

The river is flowing, the river is going.[21]
It puts its neck under a root and pulls it out.
This was the oracle pronounced for a thousand initiates,
who thought that the Ifa nuts were nothing but palm kernels.
The thousand initiates who regarded Ifa as mere palm kernels
shall yet follow Ifa.

The Moslems are still lying:[22]
they say: 'We are fasting for God every year.'
Why do you fast for God?
Do you believe God is dead?
Do you believe he is ill?
Or perhaps sad?
Olodumare[23] is never ill, and he can never be sad.
We shall never hear of his death,
unless the liars lie.

Oloirekoire Olorunkorun
consulted the oracle for one hundred and sixty-five palm trees.
He asked them to sacrifice, lest their children should be abducted.
But they refused to sacrifice.
Then the birds came and ate their fruit and scattered them.
And the rats came likewise and ate their fruit and scattered them.

The foot of the snake is not split into two.
This was the oracle for Osa,
who went through the world alone.
They washed the leaves for Osa,
they sacrificed two pigeons and also two snails.
Then one became two and Osa had children.

Raven and owl are names for Orunmila.[24]
Protector of the city is the name of Eshu.
Money sits on the head.
Debt hangs round our neck.
Nakedness clings to our bottom.
Today dear mother, the oracle is favourable to us:
Let me have money to sacrifice to my head.
Let me have money to buy the debts off my neck.
Let me have money to cover my nakedness.

Young ones never hear the death of cloth,
Cloth only wears to shreds.
Old ones never hear the death of cloth.
Cloth only wears to shreds.
Young ones never hear the death of Olodumare,
cloth only wears to shreds.
Old ones never hear the death of Olodumare,
cloth only wears to shreds.

Ogbe was hunting in the bush.
He was told to sacrifice to avoid disaster,
but Ogbe would not sacrifice.
When rain beat him hard
he sought shelter in a big hole.
Was it a tree hole? Was it an ant hole?
No, it was the anus of an elephant.
The elephant closed his anus:
Ogbe prayed but could not escape.
His relatives searched for him in vain.
Then they went and brought the sacrifice,
the same sacrifice Ogbe had refused.
Then the elephant passed him out with his excreta.

The lord of the forest and the lord of the savannah
wanted to seduce Beloved, the wife of fire.
They were asked to sacrifice broomsticks, a hen and Ifa leaves.
But the lord of the savannah refused. He said:
'And why should I, chief of the savannah, bring sacrifice,
merely because I seduced a woman?
Have I not got an army of poisonous yams and thorny shrubs
all ready to protect me?'
But the lord of the forest went and sacrificed.
The day came when Beloved, the wife of fire,
went to the house of savannah.
Then fire ran to the house of savannah and cried: 'Beloved, Beloved!'
And he burned the poisonous yams and thorny shrubs
and all the savannah was burned.
But when fire went to the forest
they sprinkled the Ifa leaves on it and it died.

This is the oracle of a hunter
who went hunting in the forest of Onikorogbo.
They asked him to sacrifice
so that he might not meet his death.
They asked him to sacrifice eggs,
all the eggs in the house.
But he refused to sacrifice.
He came into the forest,
but he found no animals to shoot.
When he had wandered about for a long time,
he met death.
For a while they were hunting together.
At last they found two eggs.
Death said to the hunter:
'You may take them home.'
The hunter proposed to divide them,
but death refused.
The hunter went home lonely.
Soon after that, famine came.
The hunter cooked the eggs
and ate them with his children.
Then death arrived and said:
'I have come for my share,
there is famine in heaven.'
The hunter said: 'Alas,
we have already eaten the eggs.'
Then death killed the hunter and his children.

There is no pregnant woman[25]
who cannot give birth to a father of secrets.
There is no woman
who cannot give birth to Orunmila himself.
If a father has begotten a child –
however long it may take,
the child may yet beget the father.
If a mother gave birth to a child,
she can still be reborn by that child.
This is what the oracle said to Orunmila
who said:
'I shall bring heaven to earth
and earth to heaven.'

Wisdom is the finest beauty of a person.
Money does not prevent you from becoming blind.
Money does not prevent you from becoming mad.
Money does not prevent you from becoming lame.
You may be ill in any part of your body,
so it is better for you to go and think again
and to select wisdom.
Come and sacrifice, that you may have rest in your body,
inside and outside.

Orifusi, the father of Elu, wanted to overcome death,
so that he might not kill him with his wives and children.
Ifa said to him:
'If you do not want death to kill you,
you must sacrifice.
But if you do not add good character,
your sacrifice shall be in vain.
Free the fowls in your basket.
Do not kill anything from today on.
Anybody who does not want death to kill him
let him not kill anything either.'

Iwori wotura.
Anybody who sees beauty and does not look at it
will soon be poor.
Red feathers are the pride of the forest.
Young leaves are the pride of the palm tree.
Iwori wotura.
White flowers are the pride of the leaves.
A swept verandah is the pride of the landlord.
Iwori wotura.
A straight tree is the pride of the forest.
A fast deer is the pride of the bush.
Iwori wotura.
The rainbow is the pride of heaven.
A beautiful woman is the pride of her husband.
Iwori wotura.
Children are the pride of their mother.
Moon and stars are the pride of the sun.
Ifa says:
'Beauty and all sorts of good fortunes arrive.'

MAGIC FORMULAS[26]

BORN TO DIE[27]

Death catches the hunter
in a net of pain.
Eshu traps the herbalist
in a sack of evil.
Shonpona carries his children away
when he dies.
The calabash is invisible
but its medicine can kill two hundred people.
The black soil of the farm is of the world[28]
but the red soil in the grave belongs to Heaven.
You my child,
Oludande,
Born-to-die,
return from the red soil of Heaven,
come and eat the black soil of this world.

(incantation to induce the reincarnation of a dead child)

RAIN MAGIC

Gentle breeze is the father of rain.
Soft wind is the father of cloudburst.
Rain will not drench me today;
rain will pack its belongings and go away.
The antelope is humming,
the buffalo is grumbling,
the pig grunts in its belly.
Words have angered the red monkey,
but today he was given the right words
and his anger will disappear.

(incantation to stop rain)

RAIN MAGIC II

The soft breeze sways the trees on the farm.
The gentle wind makes the leaves tremble:
Woya woya woya.
You cannot use a banana leaf to kill a snake.
You cannot use a stick to kill hunger.
If you want to kill wind
you cannot use Shango, you cannot use Obatala.
If you want to kill wind
you ask Oya,
and the Iroko leaf
shall not fall on the horse's back.

EVIL ON THE CROSSROADS

I look to the right:
two hundred elephants raise clouds of dust.
I look to the left:
two hundred buffaloes knock their horns together.
I look straight ahead:
two hundred weaver birds scatter –
piripi japi japi.
Death is the forest
dressed in black.
Midnight is the cloud
that darkens the earth.
Danger is waiting on every side,
but the bold oracle priest
can control two hundred elephants.
The bold medicine man
can resist two hundred buffaloes.
The bold *sigidi* spirit
can handle two hundred weaver birds.

(incantation to prevent evil on the crossroads)

WITCHES

One day the coffin comes to town
and we must sacrifice a man to it.
The coffin comes to pronounce
the sentence of the mothers:[29]
those who kill without war,
those who are blessed at midnight,
those who gnaw flesh from the belly,
those who eat liver and heart.
Neat little birds,
they sleep on their backs
and stare at the sky.
They hold the cleft stick,
they eat liver and do not vomit.
But you Abolubode, protector of kings,
you shall survive the birds and the mothers.
Four hundred and twenty hoes,
one thousand two hundred matchets
conspired against the hill;
but the hill could not be eaten,
nor could it be drunk.

(protection from witchcraft)

KNOTS

However hard you look
you will not find God on top of a palm tree.
However bold you are
you cannot fight the spirit of the Iroko tree.
However strong you curse
it shall not hit me,
your words shall return to your belly.
If you curse my head,
may you go to Heaven and leave me unharmed.
When the coucal calls for rain,
he will get wet himself.
When the parrot collects red feathers,
he will carry them in his own tail.
When the crown bird collects firewood,
he will carry it on his own head.
If you curse me –
may you carry it on your own head.

FORGIVENESS

The thorn bush will not prick its own belly.
The thorn tree will not sting its own foot.
When the hornbill sees the farmer he will laugh.
If I have wronged you, may you laugh also.
Forgive me:
the child's top is dancing on the ground,
the ant lion dances under the surface.
Will the gods reject kola nuts?
Will the king reject salt?
Forgive me, forgive me,
I am a little child.

QUARREL

Nobody will quarrel with the woodcock
because of his blue coat.
Nobody will quarrel with the parrot
because of his red tail.
You old people of this world,
don't be my enemies.
Would you kill a dog because it barks?
Would you kill a ram because he butts?
Would you kill the goat because he fucks his mother?
Forgive me, don't fight,
and let me interpret the world
like the fly that tastes the wine.

MONEY

Hunger cannot kill the fingernails before evening.
Hunger cannot kill the fingernails before noon.
Scratch your head,
scratch your neck,
come and give me good luck today.
There is no day when the sun will not rise.
There is no day on which the creator of chalk
will not create the whiteness of money.
Look after the money in your hand,
come and give me my share
of the savings club today.

MONEY II

Drizzle
outside my house.
Drizzle
falling slowly like coins
outside my house.
The thief is hiding
in the shadow of the wall.
Let him go out and gather money for me
from the hands of women.
Let me lie here like a viper:
and food will walk straight into my mouth.

POPULARITY

You cannot dispute the savannah with the buffalo.
You cannot dispute the bush with the rat.
A small child cannot beat its mother.
An old man cannot be angry with his own shit.
Why should anyone be angry with me?
Can a woman see a penis without happiness?
Why aren't you happy when you see me?
The children are enjoying themselves with the birds.
Children of the house, elders of the house,
men, women, young and old,
whoever sees a new born baby must be happy.
I am now a new born baby:
come and dance with me.

LUCK

I am waiting at the crossroads.
I look to the right –
there is nothing.
I look to the left –
there is nothing.
I look straight ahead –
there is silence.
I take the guinea pepper in my mouth.
I recite the old incantations.
I walk a little while – I see a calabash.
I break it – there is a crown of brass.
I want to pick it – it says 'No!
But you may ask for six things.'
I say, you crown of brass,
let me have money,[30]
        wife,
                child,
                        health,
                                victory,
let me return to try another life.

WEALTH

No one can twist the leopard's arm.
No one can stop the masquerader in his path.
No one can attempt to strike God.
The dead man's teeth
have to be wrenched open by force.
But palm kernels
can be plucked gently from the palm tree's neck
and every year
they will be gathered and crushed.

MEMORY

Whatever I am taught,
let me remember it.
When the big fish comes out of the water
we can see the bottom of the pond.
When the big toad comes out of the water
we can see the bottom of the well.
When the kingfisher dives into the water
his brain becomes clear.
When the cheeks of the pregnant antelope were marked,
her child was also marked.
If there is one piece of meat left in the pot
it will surely be taken by the spoon.
Everything the landlord does
is known to the swallow.
Everything that is in your brain, my father,
let it be known to me.

COURT CASE

The black goats
are holding their secret meeting
behind the ram's back.
Their tails are swishing.
The day the butter meets the fire
its life comes to an end.
The day the shit sets eyes on the ground
its life comes to an end.
But who can call death down from Heaven
to be accused in court?
My enemies in the house,
my enemies in the street,
I'll catch them under a large pot:
pirigidi!

SNAKE BITE

The snake has beauty in its tail
and pain in all its body.
The snake goes to Ejiogbe and says:
'The owner of twenty slaves is eating,
the owner of thirty servants is eating,
but I have nothing to eat.'
Ejiogbe goes into the house
and returns with eight needles.
'These are the last eight needles
and each of them carries pain.
Anyone who crosses your path,
you might sting with these needles.'
Then the snake stings Ejiogbe's child.
Come and take away the pain of the needle,
come and replace it with the sting of onion.
Don't let it sting him,
don't let it burn him,
all is in your hand, Ejiogbe.

DEATH[31]

THREE FRIENDS

I had three friends.
One asked me to sleep on the mat,
one asked me to sleep on the ground,
one asked me to sleep on his breast.
I saw myself carried on a river.
I saw the king of the river
and the king of the sun.
I saw a palm tree[32]
so weighed down with fruit
that the tree bent under the fruit,
and the fruit killed it.

THE LEOPARD

The eyeballs of the leopard are like fire.
The tail of the leopard is never at rest.
But the most powerful are his claws –
the hidden ones!

DEATH

I cannot carry it,
I cannot carry it.
If I could carry it,
I would carry it.
When the elephant dies in the bush,
something is carried into the house.
When the buffalo dies in the forest,
something is carried into the house.
But when the mouse dies in the house,
something is thrown into the bush.

FUNERAL SONGS

I say arise
but you will not rise.
If Olu is told to rise,
Olu will rise.
If Awo is told to rise,
Awo will rise.
The newly married wife
will rise when she is asked,
although she does not dare
to call her husband by name.
The elephant rises in the morning,
the buffalo rises in the morning.
The elephant lies down like a hill.
Alas, the elephant has fallen
and can never get up again!
You say you have neither wealth nor children,
not even forty cowries with which to buy salt.
You drowsy head, arise!

Had I known the elephant would fall in twenty years' time
I would have run to tie its tail.
Had I known the elephant would sleep in thirty months' time
I could have run to tie it down.
An elephant is dead and gone.
I do not see my father's face,
he has gone beyond the reach of my arm.
The house post we lean against
is being destroyed by white ants.
To whom can we go with our complaints?
Whom can we trust with our secrets?
Abandon, abandon!
Do fish abandon the water?
May your spirit never abandon this house.

Come nearer home,
mother of Aina.
O mother,
you knew how to bear children
but never learned to chide them.
Come and receive the sacrifice
from your beloved children.
You people of the road,
where did you meet her?
Mother of Kujusola,
mother of Alawede,
they met her on the road to Ede.
I thank the trees
that did not fall on her,
I thank the river
that did not carry her away.
Her head and feet covered –
like a newly married bride –
my mother travels on the underground path
and none can bar her way.

Slowly the muddy pool becomes a river,
slowly my mother's disease becomes death.
When wood breaks, it can be repaired.
But ivory breaks forever.
An egg falls to reveal a messy secret.
My mother went and carried her secret along.
She has gone far –
we look for her in vain.
But when you see the Kob antelope[33] on the way to the farm,
when you see the Kob antelope on the way to the river –
leave your arrows in the quiver
and let the dead depart in peace.

When the farmer dies
he leaves poverty to his hoe.
When the hunter dies
he leaves poverty to his bow.
When the blacksmith dies
he leaves poverty to his bellows.
When the bird dies
it leaves poverty to its nest.
Now you have died
and leave darkness to me.
Where are you now?
Are you the goat nibbling the grass around the house?
Are you the lizard, immobile in the afternoon sun?
If I tell you not to eat earthworms
it is like asking you to go hungry.
But whatever it is they eat in Heaven –
partake the meal with them.
A dead body cannot receive double punishment:
if you have no cloth to cover yourself with,
you will surely have earth to cover yourself.

MARRIAGE[34]

RECITATION OF THE BRIDE

Those who stand – let them stand well.
Those who stoop – let them stoop well.
Those who sit on the verandah – let them receive our thanks.
You the elders, who have come from far,
I thank you for honouring this day.
I pounded yam softly,
I offered it to Eshu[35] the trickster,
Eshu refused to eat.
I prepared yam flour softly,
Eshu refused to eat.
Then I asked him:
'Will you stay indoors or outside?'
He said: 'Outside.'
When the dead come looking for me,
they will meet Eshu outside.
When disease comes looking for me,
it will meet Eshu outside.
But when a child comes looking for me,
it will meet me in my room.
When I left my house
my father told me:
'Don't go through the market.'
I said: 'But why?
Are you in debt?
Do you owe the butcher?'
When I left my home
my mother told me:
'Don't go through the market.'
I said: 'But why?
Are you in debt to the salt seller?'
You people of the world,
help me to thank my mother,
for she decked me out in clothes
rich enough

to make Olokun[36] jealous,
Olokun, god of the sea.
My mother dressed me
in clothes so rich
I could confuse a god.
I am like a beggar woman
turned into a king's daughter.
They wanted to lead me to my husband's house
like a sheep to the market.
But my mother said I should be escorted
like a free born child.
Let everybody thank my mother:
she did not allow me to borrow dresses
from those who would abuse me later.
And you, my friend Ilajue,
you my best friend:
this sudden marriage has spoiled
many things for us.
We have been abusing people together,
we have been scorning together and laughing,
good things and bad, we never did them alone.
They say that marriage brings happiness
greater than any known before.
But were they thinking of you?
And you my parents:
when you don't see the river
will you forget the waves?
When you don't see the thunder
will you forget the rain?
When you don't see me any more –
will you forget me?
Is it not you who decide
when a child is old enough to have a quiver?
Is it not you who decide
when a child is old enough to have an arrow?
It was you who decided
that I was old enough

to move into another house.
Don't leave me alone in that place.
What I am about to do
you have done it yourselves with success.
Then let me succeed also.
If you don't know an elephant,
at least you hear his voice.
If you don't know the sea,
at least you have tasted salt in your soup.
If you don't know me: don't you hear my voice?
I looked right
but I saw no tree
taller than the silk cotton tree.
I looked left
but I saw no tree
taller than the silk cotton tree.
I looked in front of me
but I could not see anyone
who resembles my father.
What kind of god created me
in a sickly town
to make my relatives die like rotten yams?
If luck is not against me
I shall have them back[37]
where I am going.
If luck is not against me
they shall re-enter the world
through me.
May luck not turn against the mother.
When luck turns against the hunter
the animal escapes.
When luck turns against the farmer
his land does not yield.
When luck turns against the mother
she will bury her children
as if she were planting yams.
It is not my head that is bad,[38]

only fate.
My head – which is wearing a bright scarf today –
will surely give me
male and female children.
By this time last year
my husband was writing angry letters.
By this time last year
he was writing fighting letters.
But when this year came
he tore up his letters.
I am afraid –
not because I am a coward.
I am afraid –
not because I cannot fight.
It is this strange house
that is upsetting me.
Don't bathe me in medicines.
Forget about your charms.
My mother's care is enough for me.
I honour the bitter kola nut,
for through it I will gain Shango's favour.
I honour the red kola nut,
for through it I will gain the favour of the other gods.
I honour the red pepper –
for it cures sickness.
Those who gather firewood in the forest
tie their sticks together in bundles.
But if they tie three melons together
will they succeed?
Children of this world!
No one shall succeed in tying me.
Don't underrate the Oyoyo soup
because it is black.
It is a sweet soup.
Don't underrate me
because I am black,
because I was born by a man

who is known by two hundred people.[39]
And today
fortune descends on my head.
The melon seed soup only offends the hungry man
who was not invited to the feast.
The smell of fried bananas only offends the hungry man
who was not invited to the feast.
I who have come to this world
with ripe breasts
I have offended my younger sisters.
Whom shall I turn to in this new house?
In the strange corridors I never walked?
In the strange doors I never entered?
Whom can I turn to in this strange house?
Some of them may say:
'See a loose girl coming.'
Let them talk today –
for tomorrow they shall be silenced.
Today is a glorious day.

COMMENTS[40]

PAGIDARI

Pagidari – wood is breaking!
The tree that falls in the farm
does not kill people in the house.
The ceiling that crushes down in the bedroom
does not kill people in the street.
If the ulcer never kills the person who's got it,
he who is washing it will never be ill.
The man lying down cannot fall,
the tree lying down casts no shadow.
Death claims many victims this year.
But since we were not born together,
why should we die together?

TRICKS

The star is trying to outshine the moon,
the frog is preparing a trick to get wings,
the one who wears a cotton dress pretends to wear velvet,
the one who is wearing velvet pretends to be a king.
We all try to do
what God never intends us to do.
Watch out: 'We shall catch and kill'
is what we cry when we go to the battlefield.
We tend to forget that we shall meet another man there
uttering the same cry.
When death is far away,
we may protect our child with *aja* charm.
When death arrives,
he tears the *aja* from his neck
and carries the child along.

LAZY NEIGHBOUR

The owner of yam peels his yam in the house.
A neighbour knocks at the door.
The owner of yam throws his yam in the bedroom.
The neighbour says: 'I just heard a sound,
kerekere, that's why I came.'
The owner of yam replies:
'That was nothing, I was sharpening two knives.'
The neighbour says again: 'I still heard
something like *bi* sound behind your door.'
The owner of yam says:
I merely tried my door with a mallet.'
The neighbour says again:
'What about this huge fire burning in your hearth?'
The fellow replies:
'I am merely warming water for my bath.'
The neighbour persists:
'Why is your skin all white – when this is not the harmattan season?'
The fellow is ready with his reply:
'I was rolling on the floor when I heard of the death of Agadapidi.'
Then the neighbour says: 'Peace be with you.'
Then the owner of yam starts to shout:
'There cannot be peace,
unless the owner of food is allowed to eat his own food.'

HUNGER

Hunger makes a person lie down –
he has water in his knees.
Hunger makes a person lie down
and count the rafters in his roof.
When the Muslim is not hungry he says:
'We are forbidden to eat monkey.'
When he is hungry he eats a baboon.
Hunger will drive the Muslim woman from the harem
out into the street.
Hunger will persuade the priest
to steal from his own shrine.
'I have eaten yesterday' does not concern hunger.
There is no god like one's stomach:
we must sacrifice to it every day.

THE LAZY MAN

The lazy man lies down to sleep
and covers himself with suffering.
His breast bone sticks out –
but with him Hunger is innocent.
His father will say: 'I have not borne a child.'
When he dies, let him die,
it means nothing to anyone.
The lazy man goes from house to house,
he knows where the soup is sweet.
He never fails to find out
where they sacrifice.
And when he sees the free yam,
he starts to unbutton his shirt,
he moves close to the celebrant.
When the lazy man gets tired of himself
he joins the Koran school.

CHARACTER IS BEAUTY[41]

Character is beauty.
A woman can shine
like an antelope skin,
but if she has no character
she is nothing but a wooden doll.
Character is beauty.
A man can sparkle
like a fish in the water,
but if he has no character
he is nothing but a wooden doll.

LOVE

There are many kinds of love.
One love says:
If you die, I shall die with you.
Another love says:
If you buy the yam, I'll buy the soup.
The love of the husband
is different from the love of the wife.
The love of the children
is different from the love of the parents.
The love of the mother is the greatest!
'I know whom I love!
I shall marry him,
I shall marry him,
I shall marry him by force!'
The father says:
'Don't you know that he is poor?'
The mother says:
'Don't you know that he is lazy?'
'I shall marry him,
I shall marry him!
Even if you tie me like a goat
and you feed me on grass,
even if you beat me
until my body swells up –
I shall still know whom I love!'

WOMEN[42]

Women confuse our heads.
The faithful wife whom we see daily
in our house
is not as dear to our eyes
as the secret lover.

She truly needs good character,
the woman who has no relatives.
The woman who has no friends among her co-wives,
she needs good character indeed.

A man who wants to marry a mother and her daughter
will get away with it if he conducts his affairs wisely.
The mother receives her money in public,
the daughter receives her money in private.

But what about your younger days?
The old woman proclaims:
'I never had a secret lover.'
But what about your younger days?

God never did well when he failed to create me a woman:
I would dance *tadireke*.[43]
I would open my wrapper and regard my new god
who gives birth on the ground and who kills to eat.

I shall speak of the hunter who went hunting in the bush
while his wife was hunting in the streets.
Beware of the hunter's wife:
afterwards, you will blame the *magun* charm.
Do you think we use any old thing to protect our women?
Let those who care follow the hunter in the forest.
'Let me pull your wrapper!'
'Let me pull your waist band!'
'Leave me alone – you are a thief!'

MALE AND FEMALE POWER

There is competition between fire and water.
Fire chases water
and refuses to turn back.
But fire cannot maintain its glow beyond the water,
no matter how powerful fire is,
when it gets to the water
it must die.

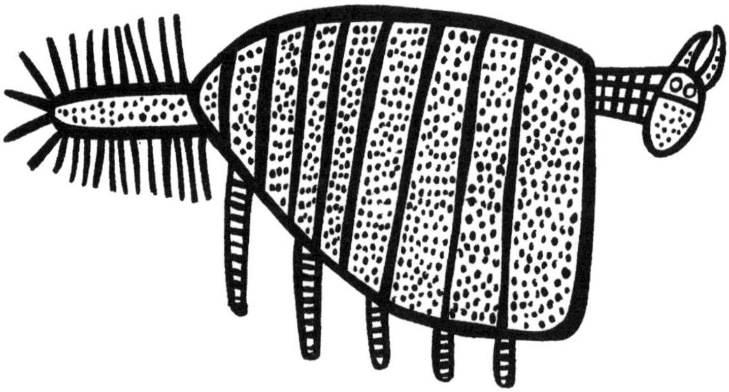

ANIMALS & PLANTS[44]

ELEPHANT

Elephant, a spirit in the bush,
elephant who brings death.
He swallows a whole palmfruit,
thorns and all.
He tramples down the grass
with his mortar legs.
Wherever he walks
the grass is forbidden to stand up again.
He tears a man like an old rag
and hangs him up in the tree.
With his single hand
he pulls two palm trees to the ground.
If he had two hands
he would tear the Heaven to shreds.
An elephant is not a load for an old man –
nor for a young man either.

HYENA

The scruffy one
who eats the meat
together with the bag
in which it is kept.
The greedy one
who eats the mother
and does not spare the child.
God's bandy-legged creature.
Killer in the night.

BUFFALO

The buffalo is the death
that makes a child climb a thorn tree.
When the buffalo dies in the forest,
the head of the household is hiding in the roof.
When the hunter meets the buffalo,
he promises never to hunt again.
He will cry out: 'I only borrowed the gun!
I only look after it for my friend!'
Little he cares about your hunting medicines,
he carries two knives on his head,
little he cares about your danegun,
he wears the thickest skin.
He is the butterfly of the savannah:
he flies along without touching the grass.
When you hear thunder without rain –
it is the buffalo approaching.

WILD BOAR

The fat one in the thick forest.
He carries scissors in his mouth,
and though we do not wish to marry his daughter,
he expects us to treat him like our father-in-law:
we must prostrate to him before we can shoot him.
A randy animal who enlarges his nose
in order to better smell the vagina.

LEOPARD

Gentle hunter,
his tail plays on the ground
while he crushes the skull.
Beautiful death
who puts on a spotted robe
when he goes to his victim.
Playful killer
whose loving embrace
splits the antelope's heart.

BUSH BUCK

Royal prince
with a mighty heart
and a mighty liver.
Your smooth neck
sways as you walk.
Descendant of kings,
must you die
to make the children of the hunter
happy?
We must not carry your body
past the king's palace.
For, if we dare, he will say:
'You have slain a royal prince,
leave him here
to be buried by me.'

DUYKER

Beautiful antelope,
you shake the grass like bells.
God has blessed you with white:
your teeth are whiter than bone,
you wash your belly with white.
God took pity on the male
when he placed your vagina at the back.
He gave you a bushy tail
to clean your vagina with.

Your thighs are worth twenty slaves,
your arms are worth thirty servants.
Anybody who kills you
will have many enemies:
he will never be able to feed
all his friends on you.
Beautiful antelope,
if you had only known
that the king was celebrating a feast,
you would have brought a little more meat.

When I kill you
I cannot be happy
until I find your body in the bush.
My pregnant wife demands your skin:
lying on it, she will bear
a beautiful child.

KOB ANTELOPE

A creature to pet and spoil like a child.
Smooth skinned
stepping cautiously in the lemon grass.
Round and plump
like a newly married wife.
The neck
heavy with brass rings.
The eyes
gentle like a bird's.
The head
beautiful like carved wood.
When you suddenly escape
you spread fine dust
like a butterfly shaking its wings.
Your neck seems long,
so very long
to the greedy hunter.

RED MONKEY

Child of maize!
Owner of the farm!
You have never borne a black child.
Your child is the colour of the farm.
Wise old man, possessor of charms!
You continue to steal,
though you are old enough not to steal.
Oh no! Since he was born,
the red monkey never stole anything:
he merely picks what he wants
in the presence of the farmer!
He does not fight the farmer:
he only stares at him.

COLOBUS

We invite him to die,
he smiles.
He dies at last,
his cheeks full of laughter.
Two rows of bare white teeth.

At daybreak
the housewife sweeps the floor,
the eagle sweeps the sky,
and colobus sweeps the top of his tree.

Abuse him
and he will follow you home.
Praise him
and he leaves you alone.
The ragged man
and the man in the embroidered gown
both covet his skin.

Lice killer
with black nails,
deep set eyes,
sweeping tail.
Too beautiful to live.
Death always follows greed.
Too beautiful to survive.
Death always follows war.

BABOON

So proud in his furry robe
he thinks he can seduce
the hunter's wife.
He rolls his eyes,
his fingernails are golden,
he has carved himself
a fine long mouth.
Sitting on top of the tree
he teaches the dog to hunt.
He pelts the farmer
with his own fruit.
He collects creepers
to pay his bride price.
Father of many children
whose wife's breasts
are never at rest.
Destroyer of our farms,
you pile the corn into the sack
of your mouth.
Four hundred when coming,
one thousand two hundred on your return.
You say:
'I am restraining myself today:
if this were not my in-laws' farm,
then trees would fall on trees
and palm trees would fall on palm trees.'

VIPER

The viper lives in the forest.
Not even the worshipper of Ogun,
the god of iron,
can pick it up.
Viper's child is beautiful
lying in its nest.
But Nini is the most beautiful of snakes.
Viper is hot with jealousy.
Let Nini then change its colour,
let it go home
and bring some colour for viper.
Viper owns the forest full of rats.
Viper owns the forest full of bush.
Viper owns the forest full of vipers.
If there is no rat, what will viper kill?
If there is no rat it will kill a mouse.
If there is no mouse it will kill a shrew.
There is no one to stop it from killing a man.
Viper!
Poisonous death,
poisonous viper,
beautiful death!

PYTHON

Swaggering prince,
giant among snakes.
They say python has no house.
I heard it a long time ago
and I laughed and laughed and laughed.
For who owns the ground under the lemon grass?
Who owns the ground under the elephant grass?
Who owns the swamp – father of rivers?
Who owns the stagnant pool – father of waters?
Because they never walk hand in hand,
people say that snakes only walk singly.
But just imagine,
suppose the viper walks in front,
the green mamba follows,
and the python creeps rumbling behind –
who will be brave enough
to wait for them?

CHICKEN

One who sees corn and is glad.
Happily eating the worm
unaware of her fate.
Every fool will be buried in the cheek.
The foolish chicken has many relatives:
oil is her uncle on the mother's side,
pepper and onion are her aunts on the father's side,
pounded yam is her in-law.
If she does not see her friend salt for a day
she does not sleep peacefully.

BUSH RAT

Okete, rat with round thighs.
Its skull is as hard as a nut.
It clears the farm –
ready to plant its own crop.
It rises on its hind legs,
it peeps around carefully:
a Muslim praying on an anthill.
Its fingers squeeze the palmfruit.
Its hand sticks out of the okra soup.
A prince who leaves troubles behind
when he says goodbye.
A prince who leaves accompanied by shouting!
They cry: 'The bush rat escapes, the bush rat escapes!'

BLUE CUCKOO

The blue cuckoo
lays white eggs in the bush.
When war captures the town
the blue cuckoo cries:
'Kill twenty, kill twenty!'
The red-bellied coucal cries:
'Kill thirty, kill thirty!'
Then death will not fail to come,
then death will not fail to come.
When men begin war,
the blue cuckoo cries:
'Fools, fools!'
The red-bellied coucal cries:
'The world is spoiled, the world is spoiled!'
Then death cannot fail to come,
then death cannot fail to come.

NEW YAM

Cassava and maize are only the poor relations of yam.
Yam is a warrior who brings strife wherever he goes:
the children quarrel for the biggest portion,
the landlord complains it was not pounded smooth like yesterday.
To plant yam is costly – but it amply repays its own debt.
You put the yam to bed in the ground,
it will bring you money
that will plant you on top of a beautiful woman.

CASSAVA[45]

Plant me like a good farmer
and I will grow fat like a yam.
Throw me away
and I will still develop well.
Only the one who hangs me on the branch of a tree
is truly my enemy.
I do not fight the one who holds the stick,
only the one who holds the pot.
When people see cassava lying by the road side,
they argue:
Is it a new wife? No, it is cassava.
See how it rubs its body with red camwood.[46]
Cassava with the rough skin on its back.

BALLADS[47]

THE MYSTERY TREE AT ERIN

No day is as sweet as the day when a tree fell down.
A huge tree fell across the road at Erin.
All the bold young men of Erin set out
and they brought their axes to cut the tree.
The tree shouted 'Ka' and the tree shouted 'Ko',
something inside him went *winrin winrinrin*,
strange noises were heard in his belly.
And the young men had water in their bottoms.
They threw down their axes and ran back to town.
Then the old men of Erin set out on their way
and they carried their axes to cut down the tree.
And when their axes crashed on the trunk,
the tree once again said 'Ka' and said 'Ko',
and they dropped their axes and ran back home.
They went to their king – but the words stuck in his throat.
In the end the king's wife was wiser than the king.
'Put two and three together', she said,
'and go and consult the oracle priest.'
And they went to meet the father of secrets
and they found him on his farm.
'Choose a deaf person', he said, 'put the axe in his hand,
send him out to the tree and he'll finish the work.'
When the deaf person started to cut the tree,
it shouted 'Ka' and it shouted 'Ko',
strange noises came out of his belly.
But the deaf man landed his axe on the trunk,
for he had no ears to hear.
The tree said *winrin winrinrin* again,
the tree shouted 'Ka' and said 'Ko'.
But the deaf man cut
and he cut the tree and it shivered and screamed
until suddenly
it was transformed into shining brass and red coral.

THE BALLAD OF KUDJOYI

I will sing of Kudjoyi,
son of Otero,
who was killed by the whims
of his wife.
It was his wife who told him:
'Every farmer's wife
wears ivory bangles,
what about me?
Kill me the largest elephant
in the whole forest.'
Kudjoyi dipped his hand
into his medicine bag.
Then smoke came from his nose
and flames shot from his mouth.
Then he set forth into the forest
of Refurefu.
He found no elephant there,
but when he got to Alawijare forest
he saw an elephant huge as a hill
even when lying down.
The elephant piled up
three heaps of sand,
and sticking palm leaves into them
he warned Kudjoyi to retreat.
Kudjoyi said:
'Unless the god of the oracle
will forsake the soothsayer,
unless Allah will forsake the Mohammedan –
I will never turn back.'
Then Agiri the elephant
who carries his spurs in front,
who builds a city wall single handed,
who pulls down two palm trees
with only one hand,

then Agiri gripped Kudjoyi and lifted him up
and carried him high in the air
into Iwo town.
Then Kudjoyi cried out: 'Come to my rescue.'
But they replied:
'When you killed the antelope and the bush buck,
did you invite us to share in the feast?'
and again Agiri the elephant lifted him up
and he carried him high into Ibadan town,
whose inhabitants are eaters of snails.
And Kudjoyi cried out to them:
'You sons of warriors
who fought Ilorin and Ijebu,
will you or will you not come to my help?
You heroes of the battlefield,
who kill on the right and kill on the left,
will you or will you not come to my help?'
But they replied:
'When you killed the antelope and the bush buck,
did you invite us to the feast?'
Then Agiri the elephant lifted him up again
and at the foot of Alo hill he placed Kudjoyi down.
He tore off his right arm and his right leg.
He tore off his left leg and his left arm.
Thus he killed Kudjoyi who never returned home again.
Kudjoyi, son of Otero,
who was sent to his death
by his wife.

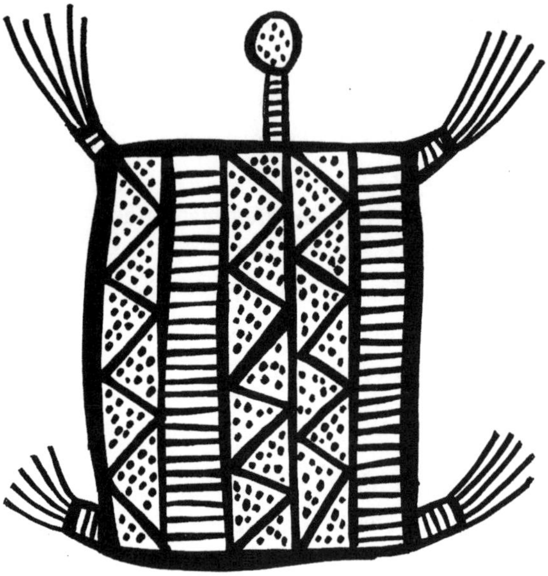

CHILDREN'S SONGS[48]

THE MOON

The moon cannot fight,
sun leave him alone.
The moon cannot fight.
Sun leave him alone!

The moon gives the earth his good light.
Come and eat bean cakes with us at midnight.
Thief! Thief with the goggle eye!

HUNGER

Hunger is beating me.
The soapseller hawks her goods about.
But if I cannot wash my inside,
how can I wash my outside?

DUCK

Duck, you are merely boasting.
You have born children.
But you have no back to carry them!
Duck, you are merely boasting.

RAIN

The rain showers down.
The earth is getting cool.
All the birds on the farm are crying:
'Sheee-ooo, sheee-ooo, sheee-ooo!'

YAM

Yam, yam, yam,
you are of pure white.
You have a gown of meat.
You have a cap of vegetables.
You have trousers of fish.
Yam, oh yam, oh yam.

BOASTING

I am the owner of my arm,
if it breaks – let it break.
I am the owner of my eye,
if it goes blind – let it go blind.
I am the owner of my belly,
if it bursts – let it burst!

THE HEN

Hen you are a warrior.
Hen you are a warrior.
Hen you are the avenger
who puts an end to the arrogance of the cockroach.

LULLABIES

Be quiet child and do not cry.
I shall bring you a big toad
from our farm in Awututu.
Be quiet child and do not cry.

Do not cry my child,
your mother went to the farm
with her big breast:
do not cry my child.
Soon she will return,
with her big breast.

Why should you weep Olukorondo,
a thorn never pricks a child's foot.
Don't I carry you on my back?
Why should you weep Olukorondo.

Where is Taiwo?[49]
Where is Taiwo?
Taiwo is at home.
Let him not be too hot,
let him not be too cold,
princely manners,
princely manners
Taiwo shall have.

HOUSETRAINING A CHILD

Lagbada shits in the house.
We do not blame him.
Lagbada pisses in the house.
We do not blame him.
But the flies will give him away.
The flies will give him away.

WORU[50]

Woru oh, Woru oh, on the farm.
Woru oh, Woru oh, on the river.
Woru who feeds birds with maize.
When I returned home I complained to my father.
Father beat Woru hard.
Under the banana tree, under the orange tree,
how did you get under the pepper shrub?
Woru bells belong to Oshun.
Oroguegba bells belong to Orisha.
Sekeseke is for Ogun.
Ask the chief for flour
to strew on the market place.
We are all children of Ogun.

SONG FOR KORI, GOD OF CHILDREN

Kori, god of little ones.
The oil pot belongs to the seller,
but the spoon belongs to Kori.
If it were not for the children,
Kori would be dead in the bush.
Olukori, let us go home.
Rain does not respect us.
Let it rain, let it rain,
we brought cloth to cover our heads.
Olukori, let us go home.
Crowned heads do not sleep in the open.

SONG OF EGBE, THE CHILDREN'S MASK SOCIETY[51]

We assemble under a great shade tree.
It is a hot shade.
They killed the cock in their mouth
and said: 'Rain will beat you!'
No rain can beat us as long as Egbe exists.
We belong to Egbe. Listen to us, Egbe.
Companions must know each other.
Akanbi show me my Egbe.
Nobody shall dare to mock us.

SONG ABUSING DRUMMERS

If it were not for the sake of the king
I would have torn your drum!
I am speaking now and you come
beating your drum *ke ke ke*.
If it were not for the sake of the king
I could have destroyed your drum!

WIN WIN TOROWIN[52]

Win win torowin
Atarowin.
I killed a bird on the farm,
I gave it to my mother,
she refused to eat.
I gave it to my father,
he refused to eat.
I asked: 'Who will eat?'
They said the king will eat.
The king ate and died.
On the seventh day
they sent a messenger.
I asked. 'What happened?'
He said: 'He has died.'
But if you kill me
the fly will have one eye,
the ant will bleed,
the stone will be pregnant.
The rain threatens in the sky
when it falls in tiny drops,
bury me with water.
Win win torowin.

THE BAD BIRD[52]

I killed the bad bird.
I killed Atekate.
I gave my father to eat.
He said: 'This is forbidden food.'
I gave my mother to eat.
She said: 'This is forbidden food.'
I gave the king to eat.
He seized the bird and ate it.
On the third day they sent me a messenger.
I asked: 'What happened?'
They said: 'The king has died.'
'With what kind of cloth have you buried him?'
'He was buried with the long-horned antelope.'
I bought many headties and clothes in the days of Abiodun.
Abiodun, the son of Shango, who owned much money and cloth.

SONG OF ABUSE

The one who does not love me,
he will become a frog
and he will jump jump jump away.
He will become a monkey with one leg
and he will hop hop hop away.

THE LAZY ONE

The trousers of the lazy one
cannot reach the ground.
The trousers of the lazy one
can't even reach his knee!

THE LAZY ONE CANNOT FIGHT

Look at this lazy one,
he cannot fight.
He met me on the dunghill,
he had to bite the dust,
he had to eat the dung.
Look at this lazy one,
he cannot fight.

MOCKING SONG

Fly, fly, fly,
fly like all the other birds.
But dishonesty never allows the cock to fly,
the cock with his red comb,
crowned head of all the birds.

WHO HAS BLOOD[53]

Who has blood?
        Chorus: Blood, blood.
Has a goat blood?
                Blood, blood.
Has a sheep blood?
                Blood, blood.
Has a horse blood?
                Blood, blood.
Has a stone blood?
                ……………..

THREE BIRDS[54]

Three birds came to the world
        Chorus: from Olongo.
One was as black as indigo
        Chorus: from Olongo.
One was as red as camwood
        Chorus: from Olongo.
Gently the first one puts down his tail
        Chorus: gently.
Gently the second one puts down his tail
        Chorus: gently.
Gently the third one puts down his tail
        Chorus: !!!

FINGER GAME

This one says: hunger is biting me.
This one says: Mother is not at home.
This one says: let's go to the farm and steal.
This one says: and if the farmer catches us?
This one says: go and steal; I'll stand apart.

HIDE AND SEEK

Ore o
    Chorus: Orere u
With what do they sow cloth?
    Chorus: With a needle.
What do they stick into its bottom?
    Chorus: A cotton thread!

Now we are playing hide and seek.
Let us play hide and seek.
Hey, tobacco seller!
This is your mother here,
whom I am wrapping in those leaves.
I opened the soup pot
and caught her right inside
stealing meat!
Who nails the roof?
    Chorus: The carpenter.
Who sews the dress?
    Chorus: The tailor…,

etc.

Cover your eyes,
cover your eyes,
the masquerade is coming.
Hide, hide, hide!
Shall I open my eyes?
I'll open them now now now!

ORIKI OF OJO[55]

I know the small Ojo and the big Ojo.
I know the Ojo who never rests when he comes to the farm.
I know the other one who is ill whenever he comes to the farm.
Another Ojo sits on the eggs with the fowl.
The fowl is rough – Ojo is rougher.
The fowl hatches – but Ojo does not hatch.
Ojo Olukoloye – two hundred songs are the business of birds.
Another Ojo – if you give him a chicken to look after,
he will buy yam to cook with it.
Another Ojo – if you give him slices of yam to plant,
he will buy a new cooking pot.
When Ojo is not in the house,
all the chickens thrive.
Had Ojo been there, he would have killed the mother hen.
Ojo is the one who collects contributions in the savings club,
but he never contributes.
A carrier of a thief's basket.

ORIKI OF TWINS[56]

Those who are woken up with a drum.
Those who have beautiful eyes.
I am glad to receive you.
You meet one who prepared cloth for you.
Two in a day!
Uncountable in the eyes of the co-wives,
though only two in the eyes of the mother.
They walk together.
They do not leave one another behind.
Two joined on top of a tree.
Something sweet on top of the tree.

PRAISE OF A CHILD

A child is like a rare bird.
A child is precious like coral.
A child is precious like brass.
You cannot buy a child on the market.
Not for all the money in the world.
The child you can buy for money is a slave.
We may have twenty slaves,
we may have thirty labourers,
only a child brings us joy,
one's child is one's child.
The buttocks of our child are not so flat
that we should tie the beads on another child's hips.
One's child is one's child.
It may have a watery head or a square head,
one's child is one's child.
It is better to leave behind a child
than let the slaves inherit one's house.
One must not rejoice too soon over a child.
Only the one who is buried by his child
is the one who has truly borne a child.
On the day of our death, our hand cannot hold a single cowry.
We need a child to inherit our belongings.

RIDDLES[58]

We call the dead – they answer.
We call the living – they do not answer.
(leaves)

We are going to Ife – we face Ife.
We are returning from Ife – we still face Ife.
(climbing and descending a palm tree one faces the same way)

We are pounding yam – the dog is dancing.
(dancing breasts of a woman pounding yam)

The black one is squatting – the red one is licking his bottom.
(cooking pot and fire)

Two tiny birds jump over two hundred trees.
(eyes)

The bereaved one has stopped weeping.
The compassionate friend is still crying.
(rain and the dripping leaves after rain)

A fire drops inside the river and does not quench.
(the bright orange palm fruit)

A beautiful maid in a thorny bush.
(tongue and teeth)

A pile of shit on a leaf, and covered with a leaf.
(humanity between heaven and earth)

We cut his head, we cut his tail.
He still persists in performing the ritual of his ancestors.
(cassava: any small piece cut off and thrown away will grow)

Five men with four arseholes.
(five fingers with only four spaces between them)

A thin staff reaches from heaven to earth.
(rain)

We tie a horse inside the house, but its mane flies above the roof.
(fire)

We invite him to come and warm himself in the sun – he came. But when we asked him to take his bath, he said that his death had come.
(salt)

Two children of the same mother sleep together and eat each other up before morning.
(two pieces of firewood)

A small bearded god whom we must worship kneeling down.
(vagina)

A little bush becomes a court case.
(vagina)

It has neither feet nor hands, yet it jumps into the bush.
(spit)

People run away from her when she is pregnant, but they rejoice when she has delivered.
(gun)

PROVERBS

Everybody who comes into this world must become something – only we don't know what!

The effort of forcing another man to be like oneself makes one an unpleasant person.

The hunter thinks the monkey is not wise. The monkey *is* wise – but he has his own logic.

A young man can have the embroidered gowns of an elder, but he can't have the rags of an elder.

As the leper's hand struggles to grip a needle, so the mind struggles with a difficult problem.

If you think of nothing but the irritation of the itch, nothing will prevent you from scratching to the bone.

He who shits on the road will meet flies on his return.

A man says that he will spoil your reputation and you say that he cannot succeed. If he says that you do not wipe your bottom: to how many people will you bare your bottom to prove him wrong?

Anger does not help. Patience is the father of good character.

When death is not ready to receive a man, he sends him an expert doctor.

The egg eater does not think of the pain it causes the hen.

Don't be seen counting the toes of the man who has only got nine.

You say you are going to destroy me, but have you thought of what God might do for me?

God himself drives away the flies from a tailless cow.

The small hand of the child cannot reach up onto the shelf. The large hand of the father cannot enter the narrow neck of the calabash.

If a man sees a snake and a woman kills it, all that matters is that the snake is dead.

A man is running through the forest and you ask him why. If he says: 'I just like running', don't believe him! He is either running after something or something is running after him.

The man who has married a woman without good character has married another man's wife.

You are a king and now you want to become rich – do you want to become a god?

NOTES

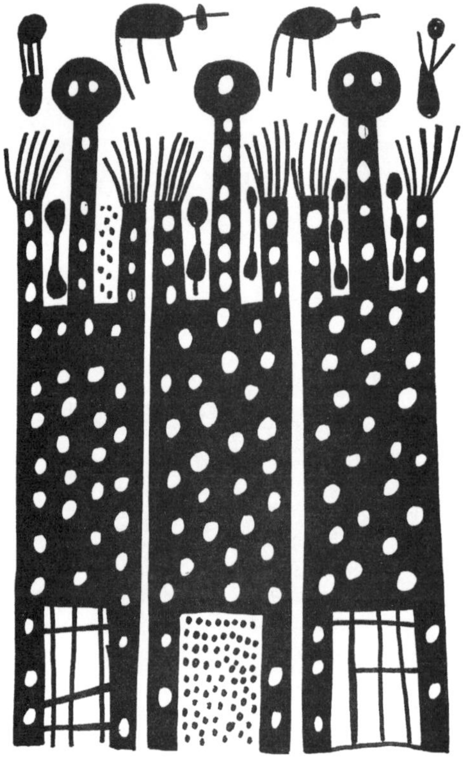

1) GODS

'Gods' is an inadequate translation of the Yoruba term *orisha*. An *orisha* is a complex, multifaceted divine being. Most *orisha* are associated with some force of nature, like thunder, storm, river, rock, or even disease. At the same time they are seen as ancestors, kings, warriors, hunters or queens, who, disillusioned with the pettiness and narrowness of mankind, transcend the boundaries of human life by turning themselves into a river or a rock, descending into the earth, ascending to heaven, or – like Shango – committing suicide by hanging. Their divine status often has to do with their suffering and disappointments on earth. The *orisha* are wild, powerful, often unpredictable, but also generous, protective and loveable.

The *oriki* (invocations) of the *orisha* are a mixture of awe, veneration, affection and familiarity. *Oriki* has wrongly been translated as 'praise-names'. Although many *oriki* are praises, other are joking abuses; some are prayers, many are simply definitions of the *orisha's* personality.

The complexity of the Yoruba *orisha* is due to a number of factors. The Yoruba people invaded the territory they now occupy in waves of immigration coming from north of the river Niger. They brought their own culture heroes with them, but they also absorbed and integrated into their world view the cults of the aboriginal populations and incorporated divinities from neighbouring peoples, like the Nupe, into their vision of the cosmos. The Yoruba talk of 401 *orisha* – a poetic way of saying there is no limit to the number of divine manifestations.

Some commentators have tried to see the *orisha* as mediators between man and God, rather like Catholic saints. This is too simplistic. The Yoruba do have a concept of a great, all powerful god, Olodumare, but he has no shrines and no priests, and there are neither rituals nor sacrifices performed for him. He is an intellectual concept which is being elaborated on mainly in the Ifa oracle. The *orisha* are conceived as different manifestations of the great god. They are all facets of the same divine substance. The Yoruba phrase 'God is a swarm of bees' highlights the ambivalence of the Yoruba concept: it provides the image of a *single* swarm which is simultaneously a collection of *innumerable* bees.

One famous myth says that at the beginning there was only one *orisha*. He is depicted as a very old man, who lived in a tiny little hut at the foot of a steep cliff. Orisha had a slave who secretly hated him. One evening, when Orisha was returning home, the slave was waiting on top of the rock and pushed a huge boulder onto the hut. Orisha was scattered into thousands of pieces. Fragments of the divine being are found in trees, rivers, rocks – and in each human being.

We cannot grasp the totality of god. We can only grasp an aspect of the divine essence. And since human beings differ, we cannot be expected to worship god in the same manner. We can only relate to the *orisha* whose divine force is compatible with the divine splinter we carry in ourselves.

Throughout their history the Yoruba people have fought wars like all other people in the world. But they have never fought a war in order to impose their beliefs on other people. They have always held the view that no human being can claim to have the whole truth revealed to him.

While I am writing this, some of the most powerful politicians in the world are trying to make us believe that the world is divided into two camps: 'good' and 'evil'. Each side claims 'goodness' and 'truth' to be their monopoly. The world might be spared a lot of suffering if we could learn something from Yoruba philosophy.

2) ESHU is the unpredictable *orisha*. He can upset the plans of gods and men. He is often called the 'trickster', but he is much more than that. He is the enemy of complacency. He teaches us that we cannot take anything for granted in life. We have to work at the relationship with our *orisha* daily: Eshu always does what is least expected and forces us to re-examine and rethink our lives. Sometimes his actions appear to be destructive, even evil. But there is a divine plan behind everything he does.

There are versions of the myth in which Orisha is smashed into thousands of divine fragments, in which it is not his slave but Eshu who rolls a huge boulder onto his hut. What appears to be an act of destruction then becomes an act of supreme wisdom: Eshu creates a universe in which plants, animals, human beings and gods are all interrelated and interdependent. Only if we accept this relationship we can survive.

The invocations of Eshu consist of a series of startling and often humourous paradoxes. Christian missionaries have demonised Eshu as 'the devil'. But this is a reflection of their own world view, which tries to neatly divide the universe into 'good' and 'evil'. The Yoruba simply cannot conceive of a creature – be it human or supernatural – that is completely evil.

The subtlety of Eshu's interference in the affairs of mankind is well illustrated by this popular story: "There were two friends who were inseparable and who never quarrelled. When Eshu heard about them, he said that it would be easy to make them come to blows. One day, when the friends were working on their fields, planting yams, Eshu was passing between them. He was wearing a cap that was white on one side and red on the other. After a while one friend said to the other: 'Who was that man walking by with the white cap?' The other replied: 'What do you mean? Have you become blind? His cap was red!' They argued for a while, but they did not consider it an important issue, so they continued planting their yams. After some time Eshu returned and walked between them again, this time coming from the other direction. Then the first friend said: 'I must apologise to you. I must really have been dreaming. Of course you were right: his cap is *red*, not white!' Then his friend really got angry, saying: 'Are you trying to make a fool of me? Do you think I no longer know the difference between red and white?' The two friends argued so fiercely that they finally began to beat each other."

Some European observers have used this story to prove that Eshu is a vicious, evil person, who maliciously destroys a peaceful relationship. In reality the story is trying to convey a very simple lesson: when two people disagree it does not necessarily mean that one of them is right and the other is wrong. They could *both* be right and they also could *both* be wrong!

3) OBATALA: Like the God of the Bible, Obatala created human beings out of clay. But unlike the Hebrew God, Obatala did not finish his creation in six days, nor did he express satisfaction with everything he had done. Obatala continues to mould every human being in the womb of the mother. He is the divine artist, and unlike the Hebrew God, he takes full responsibility for his failures. Albinos, hunchbacks and all deformed people were created by Obatala when he was drunk on palm wine – therefore they are under his special protection and they are given special functions in his shrines. It has taken Western societies a very long time before they gave handicapped people a similar status in society.

Obatala is a very ancient *orisha.* In Ede and Ejigbo there are rituals in which the high priest of Obatala is taken prisoner and later released. In Ile-Ife, the Obatala priests are driven out of town once a year, and they must live in the forest for several weeks. This could indicate that the Obatala cult existed before the Yoruba people came to settle in the land they have occupied for a thousand years.

There are many myths in which Obatala is defeated or imprisoned by other *orisha* – he is defeated by Oduduwa, he is defeated and imprisoned by Shango. But though he is no warrior, he triumphs in the end through patience, kindness and wisdom.

4) ODUDUWA: Yoruba myths may have religious, historical and even political significance. As new myths are created to reinterpret Yoruba history or to incorporate new concepts into the Yoruba world view, we may find several myths about the same *orisha* coexisting, even though they might appear to be contradictory to an outsider. Yoruba history has no book in which the sole truth – revealed by the Almighty – is fixed once and for all. Yoruba culture is flexible, adaptable to change and – since it accepts the coexistence of several parallel truths – extremely tolerant.

Oduduwa has several manifestations in Yoruba religion. In some contexts Oduduwa is the earth goddess and the wife of Obatala. In other myths, Oduduwa is a male *orisha,* a rival of Obatala. He is the *orisha* who descended from heaven on a chain and created the earth on the vast expanse of water.

In the most common and probably the most recent myth, Oduduwa is a warrior king, who led his people across the river Niger and into the land the Yoruba people now occupy. He founded the holy city of Ile-Ife, defeated the aboriginal people of the area, whom the Yoruba refer to as Igbos (meaning 'forest people'), and then invited them to settle within the walls of his city. Their king was installed as the high priest of the earth. In an annual festival the war between the Yoruba and the aboriginal inhabitants of the land and their reconciliation are still re-enacted in Ife today. Oduduwa's seven sons (some variants of the myths speak of sixteen sons) were sent out by their father to found the major Yoruba kingdoms.

Though it is fairly certain that the Yoruba people invaded their present territory in waves of migration stretched over several centuries, the myth that all Yoruba kings are direct descendants of Oduduwa is stressing a desire of the Yoruba people to see themselves as one – inspite of all the cultural differences among the various groups. Thus Oduduwa appears alternatively as mother earth, as the creator of the earth and as the conqueror of the earth. The invocations of Oduduwa in this collection refer to Oduduwa as an *orisha*, the rival of Obatala and the creator of the land.

5) OSHUMARE: The rainbow is usually associated with the python. He is said to bring both good luck and wealth. The worship of Oshumare is found primarily in the Republic of Benin. There appears to be an affinity with the deity Dan, who is worshipped by the neighbouring Fon people. I have not found priests or shrines of Oshumare in central Yorubaland.

6) YEMOJA, who is often referred to as 'the mother of fish', is associated with rivers, lakes and the ocean. Her worship was prominent in Abeokuta. Yemoja became an extremely popular *orisha* in Cuba and Brazil, because in the diaspora the ocean was the link to Africa.

7) SHONPONA is the only Yoruba *orisha* that was outlawed by the British Colonial Government. It was alleged – quite wrongly – that Shonpona priests went around spreading the disease of smallpox. Shonpona is an *orisha* associated with human suffering, particularly with the so-called 'hot' diseases, of which smallpox is the fiercest and most dangerous. Contrary to the rumours spread by Christian Yorubas, however, the priests tried to cure the disease, rather than spread it. A sudden calamity – like a man being brought down with smallpox – is interpreted as a message from the *orisha* who felt neglected. The priests are called and if they succeed to cure him, they initiate him into the cult of Shonpona. The *oriki* reproduced here were collected in Erin-Oshun by Bakare Gbadamosi. For several years, while I was living in Ilobu, I attended almost every *ose*[8] Shonpona in nearby Erin. It was a very small community of worshippers, mostly women. The *olorishas* were extremely gentle and had a passionate love for their *orisha*. They danced to a superb ensemble of *bata* drummers.

The contribution of the Shonpona worshippers to Yoruba philosophy and to Yoruba life was this: they taught people that illness is not merely a negative experience. It may force us to think more deeply about our lives, to examine our past actions and reorientate ourselves. Illness can in fact become a very positive experience if we allow ourselves to be guided by Shonpona.

---

[8] *Ose* is the ritual that is performed for an *orisha* every four days.

8) SHANGO is probably the most colourful, extrovert and extravagant of all the *orisha.* Shango was a powerful king of the kingdom of Oyo, who extended his kingdom in all directions. When his people pleaded with him to stop his endless wars, he tried to fulfil their wishes, but his generals revolted against him and he was eventually driven out of town. Disappointed with his people, he hanged himself. But his followers worshipped him and shouted: *'Oba koso!'* ('The king did not hang himself!') This is how Reverend Samuel Johnson explains the origin of the Shango cult in his *History of the Yorubas* (1921).

King Shango seemed to usurp the attributes of a much older Yoruba thunder god called Jakuta. The anthropologist Mark Schilz discovered that in some Yoruba towns in the Republic of Benin, Shango was a female *orisha,* who was worshipped as the wife of Jakuta. It is interesting that Shango priests plait their hair like women, while Shango priestesses do not kneel before their *orisha* – they prostrate like men. In most of Yoruba country 'Jakuta' has survived merely as the day on which Shango is worshipped.

The multifaceted character of Shango is demonstrated during the annual festival of the *orisha,* when one of his priests, the Baba Elegun, must go into a trance and 'carry the god on his head' for several days and nights. As soon as the spirit of Shango enters his head, the priest bursts forth in a frightening roar and a wild dance. But after this initial outburst, he entertains the public with a performance that is partly magical display of his supernatural powers and partly hilarious entertainment. The invocations of Shango celebrate his wildness and his humour, his passion and his generosity.

9) OYA is regarded as the senior wife of Shango. She is associated with the river Niger and the storm wind. In temperament she is very close to Shango. The priests of Shango and Oya both dance to powerful *bata* drum ensembles and they wear similar hairstyles and similar costumes: a short jacket studded with cowries and a skirt that consists of strips of appliqué leather that flair out during their dance.

10) OSHUN is also described as a wife of Shango, but her character is very different from Oya. Oshun is associated with the calm river that flows through Oshogbo and bears the same name. Her invocations describe her as a seductive young woman and also as an old magician. She is the main *orisha* of the town of Oshogbo, and she is given credit for the defeat of the Fulani armies outside the gates of Oshogbo. The Fulani Jihad that had destroyed old Oyo, Offa, Erin and many other Yoruba towns was halted outside Oshogbo by the powerful Ibadan army that had come to the rescue. But the Oshun worshippers know that this was not the whole story: the goddess disguised herself as a market woman who sold the Fulani soldiers poisoned food. When many of them fell ill, they were defeated by the Ibadan army.

11) ERINLE is associated with the river bearing the same name, but simultaneously he is also a hunter and a warrior. The most important centre for the Erinle cult in Nigeria was the small town of Ilobu near Oshogbo. In the early 1950s, there were twelve major shrines of Erinle in Ilobu, each named after a different spot in the river. There were nearly thirty magnificent carvings in these shrines – many of them carved by the great artist Maku. By the early 1970s the Erinle cult had died out in Ilobu and the images had long been plundered by dealers and sold to collectors. (See Ulli Beier: *Sacred Wood Carvings From One Small Yoruba Town*, Lagos 1957).

12) OGUN was the king of Ire Ekiti. Disappointed with his people he descended into the earth, but leaving behind a chain. He promised his people that whenever they were in danger, they could pull the chain and he would come and fight for them.

Ogun is a culture hero who is associated with the introduction of iron. Therefore he is associated with all those who use iron in their profession: warriors, hunters, blacksmiths, farmers, people who circumcise children or cut tribal marks, and wood carvers.

Wole Soyinka has given a fascinating reinterpretation of Ogun in his play *A Dance of the Forest*. It proves that Yoruba philosophy is by no means an archaic, obsolete world view, but that it is flexible and adaptable enough to interpret the changing world of today.

13) OSHOSI is another hunter. His worship seems to have originated in Ijebu. Oshosi is sometimes called the brother of Ogun. He is also associated with Osanyin, the *orisha* of medicinal herbs. He is not worshipped in the Ede-Oshogbo-Ilobu area.

14) AYAN AGALU: The invocations to the god of drummers refer to the hard life of the musician. He receives no salary or fixed fee for a performance. He depends on the generosity of those whose salutations he recites. Even when they are misers, he must still perform! When he leads a procession of an *orisha*, a king or a funeral, he must walk drumming for hours into the remotest corners of the town. "Blood is the pride of the healer" refers to the sacrifice that may help to cure the healer's patient. The drummer needs courage, because he alone can criticise or abuse the king in public!

15) OKE is the principal *orisha* worshipped in the town of Iragbiji. He is considered to be the husband of the river goddess Oshun, in fact they have a joint shrine in the market place of Iragbiji. The Ori Oke festival which is celebrated annually at the height of the rainy season is the main festival of Iragbiji. The priests of four *orisha* participate in the ceremonies: Oke, Oshun, Odo (another river god) and Ore (a hunter, whose worship originated in Ile-Ife). The climax of the festival is the ascent of the smooth rock that looms large over the town. The procession is led by the Aragbiji, the king of the town himself. (For a description of the Ori Oke festival see Ulli Beier: "Ori Oke Festival", in *Nigeria Magazine* 56, 1958).

16) IYA MAPO is a very ancient Yoruba deity who is the protectress of all craftswomen, especially potters, dyers and *adire* makers. Iya Mapo is an ancient earth goddess. She has neither shrines nor a priesthood, but the craftswomen have a simple annual celebration in her honour, when they dance and sing her *oriki*. Iya Mapo gives them the confidence to protect their craft monopolies. No Yoruba man is allowed to make pots, dye textiles in indigo or make batik with starch resist. (See Georgina Beier: "Yoruba Pottery", in *African Arts* May 1980; Ulli Beier et al.: *A Sea of Indigo*. Enugu/Wuppertal 1997).

17) KINGS & TOWNS

The rulers of Yoruba towns were either *obas*, that is those who could claim direct descend from Oduduwa, and were therefore entitled to wear a beaded crown, or *bales*, who were descendants of generals. In this small collection, the Alafin of Oyo and the Ogoga of Ikerre are *obas*. The Timi of Ede and the Onikoyi of Ikoyi were generals who had been sent out by the Alafin of Oyo to establish military camps to defend the borders of the Oyo kingdom. Gradually the camps grew into towns, and after some generations the generals began to rule the towns like *obas* and established a degree of independence from Oyo. Timi Laoye remained loyal to his tradition: he wore a leopard cap or, on very important occasions, a silver helmet. Only his successor, who ascended the throne in the 1970s, used political influence to obtain permission from the Oni of Ife to wear a beaded crown.

The Ogoga of Ikerre was imposed on the Yoruba town of Ikerre by the powerful Oba of Benin. The original Yoruba *oba*, the Olukerre, was given a priestly function. The Ogoga, however, wears a beaded crown, because the Oba of Benin himself claims descent from Ile-Ife and Oduduwa. Though the Bini people have a distinct language and culture, which is very different from those of the Yoruba people, both the Ife and the Benin traditions claim that the kings of Benin originally came from Ife.

The *oriki* of Yoruba *obas* and *bales* are usually recited by drummers who must be able to recite not only the *oriki* of the ruling *oba*, but the *oriki* of the entire dynasty from the founder to the present ruler. The *oriki* printed here in English translation are only short extracts from a large corpus of poetry. In the 1950s the drummers of Timi Laoye of Ede had to recite the *oriki* of twenty Timis, while the drummers of the Alafin of Oyo had to remember the poems of thirty-nine *obas*! For a more complete version see *A Short History of Ede*, Ibadan 1961, which contains the *oriki* of fifteen Timis, translated by Timi Laoye; and Ulli Beier: *Yoruba Beaded Crowns*, London 1981, which contains a selection of *oriki* of the Olukukus of Okuku, translated by Oba Olasebikan Oyewusi II.

18) IBADAN: While the rulers of Yoruba towns have their *oriki*, the towns themselves have their own invocations, known as *orile*.

The town of Ibadan had grown out of a military camp. The Olubadans (rulers of Ibadan) were mighty warriors who were able to halt the Fulani Jihad in the late 19th century. Like many invocations of Yoruba kings and towns, the *orile* of Ibadan indulge in extravagant hyperbole. (For a major study of *oriki* see Karin Barber: *I could speak until tomorrow*. Edinburgh University Press 1991).

19) ORACLE VERSES

The Yoruba people would consult the Ifa oracle before making any major decision in their lives and would ask the oracle for advice when faced with major problems like disease. The oracle priests were the custodians of a vast body of poetry called the *odu*. It was the task of the *babalawo* ('father of secrets') to find the right poem in the vast *odu* corpus that would contain the answer to his client's problem. Each *odu* was also accompanied by a prescription for a sacrifice.

For detailed information on the Ifa oracle I would like to refer the reader to the works of Wande Ambimbola, particularly *Sixteen Great Ifa Poems*, Niger 1975; and *Ifa – an Exposition of the Ifa Literary Corpus*, Ibadan 1976.

The few examples of *odu* verse included here were selected because they come across as poetry in English without requiring too much annotation.

20) "God of the Igbo": The Yoruba people called the aboriginal inhabitants of the land they occupied when they moved south across the river Niger 'Igbos', that is 'forest people'. The oracle verse that identifies Obatala as "God of the Igbo" indicates therefore that he was regarded as an ancient divinity whom the invading Yoruba adopted from the aboriginal population.

21) "The river is flowing, the river is going": this verse predicts that the sceptics will eventually recognise the truth in the Ifa oracle.

22) "The Moslems are still lying": In the 1950s, *orisha* worshippers, Moslems and Christians were still living peacefully together in the same compound. It was not until the early 1970s when Muslim states in the Middle East began to finance the construction of huge mosques in Yorubaland and when Islam became very militant, that *orisha* worshippers felt seriously threatened by Islam. The reference to Moslems found in this volume (which were collected much earlier) should be seen as a form of joking abuse. Notice that even the *oriki* of the *orisha* themselves contain joking abuse!

23) Olodumare is the supreme god.

24) Orunmila is the name of the legendary founder of the Ifa oracle.

25) "There is no pregnant woman": the oracle here predicts that an ancestor will be reincarnated through the pregnant woman who has consulted the oracle.

26) MAGIC FORMULAS

These formulas were meant to strengthen an individual's confidence and help him to face the vicissitudes of life. They were often accompanied by a small sacrifice to the person's *ori inu*, his 'inner head' that is his character or personal destiny.

27) Born to die: *Abiku*, that is 'children born to die', were spirit children who sent one of their own to be born by a human mother. The *abiku* was aware of his status and insisted on bringing sacrifices to his spirit companions. However, before the *abiku* reached the age of seven, his companions often called him back and he died. Some *abiku* were said to return to the same mother several times. This is an incantation that will induce the child to return and to stay. The name 'Duro' ('stay!') was given to children who finally stayed after dying several times.

28) "The black soil of the farm": The fertile 'black soil of the farm' is where plants grow. Digging deeper one reaches the red laterite earth in which the dead are buried.

29) "The mothers": *Aje* are powerful female spirits who are potentially destructive. They are so powerful that even the *orisha* have no power to protect you from them. The *aje* are respectfully addressed as 'our mothers'. In the *Gelede* society men dance to entertain and appease these powerful spirits.

30) "Money, wife, child": The reason why the Yoruba list these three wishes in this order is because if you have money, you can pay the bride price for a wife; if you have a wife, you can expect a child.

31) DEATH

The death of an old person who is survived by children and grandchildren is an occasion for both mourning and rejoicing, because the life has been fulfilled and the deceased will eventually return.

The death of a young child causes despair. When the mother runs through the streets, announcing the death of her child, her grief finds expression in a highly stylised form of poetry. Eventually she derives comfort from the belief that the same child will return to be reborn by her.

32) "I SAW A PALM TREE": the image of the palm tree weighed down by its fruit refers to an old person who dies, but leaves children behind.

33) "THE KOB ANTELOPE": it is believed that before the recently deceased depart to the sphere of the ancestors, they hover around the living for a while. Sometimes they may venture near them in the form of an animal.

34) MARRIAGE

When the young bride is led in procession to the compound of her husband, she is dressed up in the finest handwoven cloth and wears beads and jewellery that are family heirlooms. She is led by a group of drummers who recite the *oriki* of her family. She is in a state of great excitement: worried at the thought of leaving her home and having to adapt to a new environment; at the same time jubilant at the prospect of becoming a mother. Her chant is largely improvised.

35) ESHU: the bride here refers to the fact that a mud shrine of Eshu usually stands outside the compound to protect it.

36) OLOKUN, the god of the sea, is also revered as the god of wealth.

37) "I SHALL HAVE THEM BACK": it appears that several relatives of the bride had died recently; she now prays that they may be reborn through her.

38) "IT IS NOT MY HEAD THAT IS BAD": 'head' (*ori inu*) in the sense of personal destiny.

39) "WHO IS KNOWN BY TWO HUNDRED PEOPLE": *Omoluabi* – a highly respected person, a man of honour, sometimes defined as one who is known to and respected by two hundred people.

40) COMMENTS

The Yoruba had a travelling theatre, known as *Alarinjo* or *Agbegijo*. Their performance consisted of a mixture of classical dance, acrobatics, satirical mask and the chanting of poetry. The singers would recite the *oriki* of the important people in the audience, and they would also make witty comments on the hardships of life (hunger, famine) and on the common vices of human beings: greed, laziness, deceitfulness. The first six poems in this section are texts recorded from *Alarinjo* performers in Oshogbo and Erin-Oshun in the early '60s. This type of poetry is known as *iwi*. The section headed 'women' are *ijala*, that is hunters' poems. They are joking comments on women who have secret lovers and on the magic charm called *magun*, which the hunters use to guard their wives while they go out into the forest hunting.

41) Character is beauty: For the Yoruba, 'beauty' was not just a matter of aesthetics, it had less to do with proportion, texture and colour than with meaning. A Yoruba carving lost its significance when the *orisha*, in whose honour it was carved, was no longer worshipped.

42) Women: The hunters' poems on women were collected in the early 1960s. The banter about women's infidelity reflects a change in Yoruba mores. Adultery used to be very rare, though women who were past child bearing age often left their husband, set themselves up as independent traders and then felt free to have other relationships.

43) Tadireke: see comment in the chapter "On translating Yoruba poetry".

44) ANIMALS & PLANTS

Not only gods and men have their *oriki*, but also animals and plants. The hunters' chants describe the animals of the forest with affection and humour.

45) CASSAVA: The chanter refers to the fact that cassava is very easy to grow. Even if a piece of cassava is thrown away carelessly it will take root. The reference to the stick and the pot refers to the pounding of the cooked cassava in an earthenware pot. The one who wields the stick will not be affected, but the one who holds the pot may burn his fingers.

46) "RED CAMWOOD" is ground to a powder with which the new bride may rub her skin. The allusion here is to the reddish but hairy skin of cassava.

47) BALLADS

Long poems that tell elaborate stories are relatively rare in Yoruba poetry. Bakare Gbadamosi collected "The Mystery at Erin" from the *Alarinjo* masqueraders at Erin-Oshun and the "Ballad of Kudjoyi" from the hunters in Oshogbo. A completely different version of the "Mystery at Erin" and a much longer version of "Kudjoyi" were published by S.A. Babalola in *Black Orpheus* no. 1 (1957).

48) CHILDREN'S SONGS

Yoruba children had virtually no toys. They spent much of their time participating in the lives of adults: they followed the masqueraders and watched the performances of the Shango priests or the travelling acrobats. They worked on the farm or traded on the market. Many of them had their own religious associations and celebrated Kori, the *orisha* of children. Children who were *abiku* ('born to die') brought sacrifices to their spirit companions.

But they still found time to play, like children all over the world. A favourite game was *iyawo*, when a little girl was dressed up in rich clothes and beads borrowed from her mother, and went on the 'bride's procession' through the town, followed by chanting 'relatives' and led by boy drummers.

One of the few toys that adults made for children was a wooden doll which girls tied onto their back the way mothers carry their children. The body of the doll was just a flat rectangle with geometric designs, but the head was finely carved, with elaborate hairstyle and tribal marks.

Many of the games included songs which the children made up themselves. Other children's songs were based on historical incidents, which they had picked up from priests or hunters who chanted *oriki* or ballads. Often the real meaning was lost in their childish versions, but the fascination remained.

49) Taiwo is the name given to the first born of twins.

50) Woru: This is one of the most popular Yoruba children's songs, and it is also performed by drummers. Most Yoruba people remember singing it in their childhood, but few of them know what it is all about. I am indebted to Rowland Abiodun for this interpretation: "This poem tries to comfort parents who are worried about their restless child. Woru roams about on the farm, he plays by the river and feeds the birds with maize. One minute he hides under the banana tree, the next you find him under the orange tree. What is he up to under the pepper shrub? The father beats Woru: 'Don't play with the brass jewellery of Oshun! Don't play with the white metal bracelets of Obatala! Don't you know that Sekeseke rattles belong to Ogun?' Now he is scattering flour on the marketplace! But we are all children of Ogun. Ogun is the explorer, the adventurer, the inventor, the artist. He is a restless *orisha*, and all children have a little bit of Ogun's spirit in them."

51) Song of Egbe: *Egbe* literally means association or fraternity. In this case it refers to the children's own masquerade. The children claim that – like the adult ancestral masqueraders – they have the power to stop the rain during their ceremonies. "To kill the cock in their mouths" is a metaphor for 'to laugh mockingly'.

52) Win win torowin & The bad bird: These appear to be two garbled versions of an ancient song or maybe a drummer's recitation about the death of King Abiodun of Oyo, who was allegedly poisoned by his son.

53) Who has blood is a game in which the children are lulled into a repetitive rhythm, so that in the end one or two will repeat the chorus "Blood, blood" even after the line "Has a stone blood?"

54) Three birds: The observant child will notice that even though three birds are mentioned in the first line, the poem actually lists only two: the red and the black. It will therefore keep silent after the line "the third one puts down its tail".

55) Oriki of Ojo: Ojo is the name given to a child born with the navel chord around its neck. These *'oriki'* take the form of joking abuse.

56) Oriki of twins: Twins are spirit children and are believed to bring good luck and wealth to the family. Because of their playful cheekiness they are sometimes associated with the colobus monkey, hence "Something sweet on top of the tree". (For a collection of songs about twins see Val Olayemi: *Orin Ibeji*. Institute of African Studies, University of Ibadan 1971).

58) RIDDLES

Yoruba riddles are very hard to solve. But this is not just a guessing game: rather people compete in finding the most original and humorous poetic metaphor.

BIBLIOGRAPHY

This short bibliography and discography only includes works that are the outcome of my association with Timi Laoye, Bakare Gbadamosi and members of the Duro Ladipo Theatre Company. Other major works on Yoruba poetry are referred to in the section "Notes".

Timi Laoye I: "Yoruba drums", in: *Odu – A Journal of Yoruba Studies* (Ibadan 1959).

Ulli Beier: *A Year of Sacred Festivals in One Yoruba Town*. Special publication of *Nigeria Magazine* (Lagos 1959).
(A documentation of the festival cycle in Ede, which includes examples of Yoruba poetry.)

Bakare Gbadamosi: *Oriki*. Ibadan: Mbari 1961. (in Yoruba)

Adetoyese Laoye I: *Oriki Ati Orile*. Oshogbo: Mbari Mbayo 1963. (in Yoruba)

Adetoyese Timi Laoye I: *Oriki Awon Timi Ede*. Oshogbo: Mbari Mbayo 1963. (in Yoruba)

Ulli Beier & Bakare Gbadamosi: *The Moon Cannot Fight*. Yoruba children's poetry, with illustrations by Georgina Betts (Beier). Ibadan: Mbari 1964.

Ulli Beier & Bakare Gbadamosi: *Yoruba Poetry*. Special publication of *Black Orpheus*. Ibadan (undated, 1964?).

Duro Ladipo: *Three Yoruba Plays: Oba Koso, Oba Moro, Oba Waja*. English adaptations by Ulli Beier. Ibadan: Mbari 1964.

Ademola Onibonokuta: *Ilepa Dudu Aiye*. Oshogbo: Mbari Mbayo 1965. (Yoruba magic formulas in Yoruba)

Bakare Gbadamosi: *Oro Pelu Idire*. Oshogbo: Mbari Mbayo 1965. (Yoruba stories in Yoruba)

Obotunde Ijimere: *Eda*. Yoruba translation by Duro Ladipo: *Ti Duro Ladipo Tumo Si: Eda Yoruba Pelu Orin Ati Ilu*. Oshogbo: Mbari Mbayo 1965.

Obotunde Ijimere: *The Imprisonment of Obatala. Everyman. Woyengi*. London/Ibadan/Nairobi: Heinemann African Writers Series 1966.

Tijani Mayakiri: *Ifa – Awon Merindilogun.* Oshogbo: Mbari Mbayo 1966. (Mayakiri was a lead actor in the Duro Ladipo Theatre)

Duro Ladipo, Wale Ogunyemi, Obotunde Ijimere: *Three Nigerian Plays: Moremi. The Scheme. Born With the Fire On His Head.* London: Longmans 1967. (Ladipo's *Moremi* in Beier's English adaptation)

Ulli Beier & Bakare Gbadamosi: *Ijala – Yoruba Hunters' Poems.* Port Moresby: Papua Pocket Poets 1967.
(Limited edition used as a textbook in the literature classes of the University of PNG)

Bakare Gbadamosi & Ulli Beier: *Not Even God Is Ripe Enough.* Yoruba Stories. London: Heinemann 1968.

Der Löwe und die Perle. Four African plays translated into German by Helmut Heinrich. Berlin: Volk und Welt 1973.
(Includes *The Imprisonment of Obatala.* Another German translation of *The Imprisonment* by Jahnheiz Jahn was broadcasted on Westdeutscher Rundfunk. There was also a radio performance in Norwegian, but no details are available)

Obotunde Ijimere: *Kifungo Cha Obatala.* Swahili translation of *The Imprisonment of Obatala.* Nairobi: Heinemann 1978.

Ulli Beier & Bakare Gbadamosi: *Yoruba Poetry.* Cambridge: University Press 1970.

Ulli Beier: *Yoruba Beaded Crowns. Sacred Regalia of the Olokuku of Okuku.* London: Ethnographica 1984.
(Includes *oriki* of the Olokukus and the *oriki* of the 12 major crowns)

Ulli Beier (ed.): *Yoruba Theater. Fünf Theaterstücke aus dem Repertoire des Duro Ladipo-Theaters.* Vol. 1: *Oba Koso, Oba Waja, Moremi* by Duro Ladipo. Vol 2: *Jedermann, Die Gefangenschaft des Obatala* by Obotunde Ijimere. German translations by Ulli Beier. Bayreuth: Iwalewa 1989.

Muraina Oyelami: *Yoruba Dundun Music – A New Notation With Basic Exercises and Five Ensemble Pieces.* Bayreuth: Iwalewa 1989.

Muraina Oyelami: *Yoruba Bata Music – A New Notation with Basic Exercises and Ensemble Pieces.* Bayreuth: Iwalewa 1991.
(Oyelami was lead drummer in the Duro Ladipo Theatre Company. He has since had a dual career as musician and painter and is now

holder of the very senior chieftaincy title of Esa in his native town Iragbiji).

Ulli Beier (ed.): *The Return of Shango: The Theatre of Duro Ladipo.* Bayreuth: Iwalewa 1994.
(Contains the plays *Oba Koso* and *Moremi* in English adaptations by Beier and reviews of performances in Germany, the UK and the USA)

SELECT DISCOGRAPHY

Oba Koso & Eda: Complete performances of *Oba Koso* and *Eda* were recorded by Curt Wittig in Oshogbo in 1965.
(Unfortunately only the reel-to-reel tapes of these historic recordings survived. Extracts from *Oba Koso* and *Eda* were produced on two sides of an LP. Unfortunately the complete edition of 1000 copies that was shipped to Nigeria never arrived! Only a few advance copies survived.)

Oba Koso by Duro Ladipo and his National Theatre, recorded by Curt Wittig live in New York 1975. Kaleidophone, Washington KS 2201. Two record set, stereo.
(A brilliant performance and a brilliant recording. The comparison with the 1965 recording enables us to compare the singing and poetry chanting of different artists.)

Okuta Percussion: Osika. Arc Music 1991.
(Musicians: Tunji Beier, Rabiu Ayandokun, Ademola Onibonokuta, Terje Isungset. Includes several tracks with Yoruba chanting by Ademola Onibonokuta.)

Wole Soyinka reads Yoruba poetry with Okuta Percussion. Migila 1994, live recording at Iwalewa Haus, Bayreuth, March 11 1992.
(Musicians: Tunji Beier, Rabiu Ayandokun, Ron Reeves. Yoruba Chanting: Rabiu Ayandokan. Texts: Ulli Beier & Bakare Gbadamosi: *Yoruba Poetry.* Cambridge: University Press 1970. No attempt was made here to reproduce the effect of a Yoruba performance. Wole Soyinka's concept aims at producing a new work of art of comparable intensity and power).

THE DRAWINGS

Georgina Beier's drawings in this book are adaptations of Yoruba wall paintings. The Yoruba people have been called 'the most prolific wood carvers in Africa', but little attention has been paid to their paintings. This may partly be due to the fact that murals are relatively rare, that they are ephemeral and cannot be acquired or traded.

Wall paintings were executed on the walls of shrines; predominantly on the shrines of Obatala or deities closely related to him (*orisha funfun*). There were no professional painters who trained apprentices and accepted commissions. The artists were senior priestesses in the respective shrines. Both the inner sanctum and the outside walls could be painted. The walls were plastered with sheep's dung. Only three or four colours were used: white (from chalk), black (soot or very dark indigo), yellow ochre and a brownish red (camwood). The murals were normally renewed each year before the *orisha*'s annual festival. The walls were replastered and the new painting was carried out by the same artist, if she was still alive.

Photographs taken over the years of the shrines of Oluorogbo in Ife and of Irele in Ikirun show that successive artists use the same icons, sometimes in slightly different arrangements, but the hand of the individual artists is easily recognisable: attention to detail and the rhythm and flow of the line reveal unique personalities.

The paintings are sometimes said to carry messages from the *orisha*. But the artists are usually unwilling to name individual images and when they do, they may contradict themselves on later occasions. The Obatala shrines appear to celebrate the creativity of the *orisha*: an exuberant assembly of gods, men and animals.

The vision of the Yoruba muralists has no parallel in any other Yoruba art form: Yoruba images in wood, brass, stone or mud, each follow different aesthetic principles. The only other form of painting practised by Yoruba women are indigo starch-resist batiks (*adire eleko*). This is a relatively recent art form, which originated in the 1920s. It is carried out by professional craftswomen. In style, mood and meaning it bears no resemblance to the muralists' art. The designs, which are applied to women's clothing – wrappers and headties – have no religious significance at all. They are defined as ostrich, snake, banana, trousers and so on. The designs are stylised and highly decorative. The execution is precise and refined. By comparison the murals on shrines are much rougher and bolder. The images are unfamiliar, startling and mysterious.

The images in this book are derived from the Obatala shrine in Ogbomosho (title page, pp. 8, 28, 76, 144) and the Irele shrine in Ikirun (pp. 56, 100, 120, 166). For photographs of Yoruba wall paintings see *Odu* 8 (Ibadan 1960).

What the critics say....

„Bayreuth African Studies produces a stream of texts on African cultural issues that few British or American publishers appear able to rival... I wish to applaud the result of the endeavour"
Jane Plastow in ***African Theatre Playwrights and Politics***

„une collection riche en publications de grande qualité" Abdourahman Waberi in ***Hommes & Migration***

On BASS 30: Anglophone Cameroon Writing
„an important landmark in the critical discourse of Cameroon literature as a whole"
Teddy Ako in ***Cameroon Post***

ON BASS 31: Breitinger: Theatre and Performance in Africa
„presents an excellent array of texts, good to pass on to students and colleagues"
Gaurav Desai in ***Research in African Literature*** (USA)
„an important resource for all concerned with African Theatre"
Martin Banham in ***TheatreResearch International*** (UK)

On BASS 32 Derek Wright: *The Novels of Nuruddin Farah.*
"a landmark in the criticism of the African novel"
Jaqueline Bardolph in ***Research in African Literature*** (USA)
„an admirable first book on Farah and indispensable reading"
Journal of Commonwealth Literature (UK)
„a most reliable critic, a rigourous scholar and yet a clearly a fan of the author"
Stewart Brown in ***African Affairs*** (UK)
„ an insightful introduction to Farah's work. Chris Dunton in ***West Africa*** (UK)
„Readers of Farah are in Wright's debt for his research"
R.W. Dasenbrock in ***World Literature Today*** (USA)
„un rapporto attivo ed intelligente..con pregio di nuovi stimolanti interrogativi"
Maria Guarducci in ***Africa*** (Italy)

On BASS 39 Breitinger. Uganda: The Cultural Landscape
„Breitinger has done Isis work..gathered and remembered the scattered fragments – a rediscovered Rosetta stone" Peter Nazareth in ***World Literature Today*** (USA)

On BASS 40 Obafemi: Contemporary Nigerian Theatre
„Obafemi knows his subject very well and his passion for theatre is in no doubt"
Osita Okagube in ***African Theatre*** (UK)

On BASS 42 Wright: Contemporary African Fiction
„Wright's distinguished scholarship guarantees that the contributions are so various, engaging and scholarly" Anne Collet in ***New Literature Review*** (Australia)
„the articles demonstrate the complexity with which African writers relate to changing national landscapes and offer enlightening close reading" Cecilia Moretti in ***Review Journal*** (Australia)

On BASS 43 Kerr: Dance, Media Entertainment & Popular Theatre
„Kerr is writing provocative and thoughtful good sense"
Jane Plastow in ***African Theatre:Writers and Politics*** (UK)

On BASS 48 Arndt: African Women's Literature

On BASS 49 Rohmer: Theatre and Performance in Zimbabwe
„another welcome nail in the coffin of library based criticism of African theatre"
Jane Plastow in ***African Theatre***: (UK)

On BASS 55 Simatei: The Novel and the Politics of Nation Building
„a brilliant book" Peter Nazareth in ***World Literature Today*** (USA)

1 *The Sudan: Ethnicity and National Cohesion.* 85 pp. EUR 6.95
2 *Towards African Authenticity - Language and Literary Form.* 106 pp. EUR 6.95
3 *Littératures africaines francophones.* 122 pp. EUR 6.95
4 *Approaches to African Identity.* 90 pp. EUR 6.95 (out of print)
5 *Language and Education in Africa.* 144 pp. EUR 6.95 (out of print)
6 *Literature and African Identity.* 126 pp. EUR 6.95
7 *Drama and Theatre in Africa.* 87 pp. EUR 6.95
8 *Interviews avec des écrivains africains francophones.* 95 pp. EUR 6.95
9 *Perspectives on African Music.* 139 pp. EUR 10.95 (out of print)
10 *Douala 1893 - La Revolte des esclaves mercenaires.* 96 pp. EUR 6.95
11 *African and Western Legal Systems in Contact.* 89 pp. EUR 6.95
12 *Three Yoruba Artists.* 93 pp. EUR 6.95 (out of print)
13 *Patterns of Language Knowledge and Language Use in Botswana.* 83 pp. EUR 6.95
14 *Kulankula - Interviews with Writers from Malawi and Lesotho.* 75 pp. EUR 6.95
15 *English in East and Central Africa I.* 97 pp. EUR 6.95
16 *Essays on Music in Africa II.* 187 pp. EUR 15.95
17 *New Religious Movements and Society in Nigeria.* 82 pp. EUR 6.95 (out of print)
17 *Linguistics in the Service of Africa.* 95 pp. EUR 6.95
19/20 *Littérature et politique en Afrique noire.* 247 pp. EUR 20.95
21/22 *Yoruba Drumming. The Dundun Tradition.* 553 pp. EUR 29.95
23 *Le Champ littéraire togolais.* 200 pp. EUR 15.95
24 *English in East and Central Africa II.* 113 pp. EUR 7.95
25 *Akin Euba - An Introduction to a Nigerian Composer.* 112 pp. EUR 10.95
26 *Focus on Women in Africa.* 204 pp. EUR 15.95
27 *Survey of Zimbabwean Writers. Educational and Literary Careers.* 172 pp. EUR 15.95
28 *Koloniale Konflikte im Alltag.* 184 pp. EUR 15.95
29 *Intercultural Music.* 268 pp. EUR 20.95
30 *Anglophone Cameroon Writing.* 204 pp. EUR 15.95
31 *Theatre and Performance in Africa: Intercultural Perspectives.* 220 pp. EUR 23.95
32 *The Novels of Nuruddin Farah.* 170 pp. EUR 15.95 [EUR 23.95 cloth]
33 *Échanges Franco-Allemands sur l'Afrique.* 252 pp. DM EUR 20.95
34 *Contemporary Relativism with Reference to Culture and Africa.* 270 pp. EUR 20.95
35 *Aids-Education through Theatre: Case Studies from Uganda.* 205 pp. EUR 20.95
36 *Theatre for Development.* 80 pp. EUR 8.95
37 *The Life and Writings of Gakaara wa Wanjau.* 276 pp. EUR 20.95
38 *Primary Education and Social Integration.* 183 pp. EUR 20.95
39 *Uganda: The Cultural Landscape.* 305 pp. EUR 20.95 [EUR 32.95 cloth]
40 *Contemporary Nigerian Theatre.* 306 pp, 20 photographs. EUR 23.95 [EUR 30.95 cloth]
41 *Land Law and Land Ownership in Africa.* 260 pp. EUR 20.95
42 *Contemporary African Fiction.* 268 pp. EUR 20.95 [EUR 33.95 cloth]
43 *Dance, Media Entertainment and Popular Theatre in South East Africa.* 286 pp. EUR 20.95 [EUR 35.95 cloth]